CHRISTMAS
AROUND THE WORLD

Researched and compiled by

MARIA HUBERT

SUTTON PUBLISHING

First published in the United Kingdom in 1998
Sutton Publishing Limited · Phoenix Mill · Thrupp
Stroud · Gloucestershire

British Library Cataloguing in Publication Data
A catalogue record for this book is available from the British Library

ISBN 0-7509-1724-5

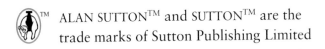 ALAN SUTTON™ and SUTTON™ are the trade marks of Sutton Publishing Limited

Typeset in 11/15 Sabon.
Typesetting and origination by
Sutton Publishing Limited.
Printed in Great Britain by
Redwood Books Ltd, Trowbridge, Wiltshire.

CONTENTS

Religious Ceremonies

Popular Traditions

Preparations and Victuals

Gift-giving and Receiving

Preparing for the church service in old Carpathia, 1888.

Traditional English Christmas

AN INTRODUCTION

Maria Hubert and others

All over the world, particularly in the New World, people think of an English Christmas as the epitome of seasonal jollification. We seem to have lost some of the feeling which helps to make Christmas what it is in our hearts and memories. Perhaps in the recent stage-sets of Victorian Christmas, we have all forgotten our own Christmases. The following account is set firmly in the immediate postwar period, which everyone over forty will remember with nostalgia as a real English Christmas!

I was brought up in Leeds in the County of Yorkshire. A baby-boomer born in 1945, my early years were a memory of ration books and bombed-out buildings. The first Christmas I can really remember was when I was six, and I was taken to the Santa grotto in Lewis's department store in the Headrow. The queue seemed to last forever, but it was worth the wait. The air tingled with a magic. We waited, over-looked by Santa's Elves to see we did not wander off, while parents made surreptitious forays into the toy department!

Every year was different – one year it was a space rocket going to the moon, but back in 1951 it was a magical sleigh ride. I can only think it was some kind of early motion simulator. You sat in the sleigh in rows, and it flew off into the skies. It must be true – you could feel it take off, and then the sky sped past the windows for what seemed like an age until you landed, a very bumpy landing in the snow at the North Pole; look, there was the North Pole outside the window! Then we all had to get out of the top door; this was important as the door we had entered was, we were told, buried in a snowdrift, and was stuck.

The grotto was everything we hoped it would be, a series of caves white with glittering frost. An elf led us all through the dark cave, showing us side caves which were hives of activity – life-size animated scenes of elves cutting trees to make another toy store for the ever-growing workshops; elves making toys and packing the sleigh – and then, on a gorgeous crimson and gold throne sat the great man himself, assisted by the Christmas Fairy, that every little girl wanted to be, in her pink and tinselled dress. We would tell Santa our most secret wishes: a walky-talky doll, a clockwork train set, a Christmas annual. Very modest by today's standards. Santa would ask us if we had been good, helped Mummy, said our prayers and added up our sums for teacher, to which of course we had always the same whispered 'yes'. Then, promising to do what he could, he would pass us to the Christmas Fairy who would tap each child with her magic wand and then tap Santa's bag – that was to make sure that each child got the gift Santa intended for him or her!

All too soon we were returned, filing out through the now 'unstuck' rear door to be deposited back with our parents – who were trying to hide huge bags – clutching our present from Santa. It did not matter to us that it was a packet of chalks and a slate, or a magic paintbook which only required water to make the pictures coloured (my favourite). What mattered was that it had been a trip of a lifetime and we were brought up to appreciate the simple things in those postwar years.

As I grew older, I began to appreciate the wonderful Christmas windows in the big stores. Always animated, often with carols and Christmas songs coming over a tannoy system. In those days the shops in all the towns saw the value in such an expense as an elaborate window, the like of which you will only find in a very few shops in London today. Shoppers who stopped to look at the windows were tempted inside by the windows, or the appealing offer of 'Christmas teas for weary shoppers'. Looking back, I can remember even the small corner shops made up a Christmas window with all their best merchandise on display among cottonwool snow and paper icicles, confident that they would make their best sales that season despite the lure of the big town shops – hadn't they a pile of 'Christmas Club' cashbooks in their safe with the accumulated savings of their customers, which would have to be spent in their shops?

They would order annuals, hams, pork pies and whole cheeses. You could buy Christmas decorations, stocking toys and boxed compendiums of games. Specially packed stockings and hankies and tobacco goods were sitting in the windows side by side with chocolates, sweets and the jars of coloured bathsalts.

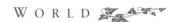

Even the florists had a healthy time at Christmas. For in my part of England it was popular to have a wreath of Christmas roses, and evergreens and hollyberries made to put on the grave of any relative who had passed on, a sign of remembrance for loved ones at this special time of year when everyone was thought about.

At the age of twelve I was allowed to catch the tramcar after school to town to do my own Christmas shopping. Most schoolchildren made straight for Woolworth's where they could, for sixpence, buy a packet of violet-scented notepaper and envelopes for granny, and many other gifts cheap enough to be bought from accumulated Carol-singing money. The Christmas-card counter sold out of the best designs daily, and often the only evidence of the glitter cards was a little sprinkling of glitter dust left on the counter. But go a little earlier and you would find cards from 1 (old) penny up to a whole shilling, loose in glass-divided bays on a long counter just inside the main doors.

By 4.30 p.m. the sky was darkening and all the Christmas lights were lit, the Salvation Army were always there playing carols by the live crib in the city square; the baked-potato stand and the hot-chestnut man were always to be found on the most populous streets, and the hot-pie-and-peas man did a roaring trade! Leeds Market was an exceptional shopping venue, this big Victorian building resounding with the cries of the different traders, and the brass band playing from the centre could be heard all around. THIS was Christmas entertainment. It was provided free by the shops and city council; it gave the public a feeling of well-being and they spent freely within their own individual limits. The spirit would spill over to the traders who would slip in an extra few oranges, or a few extra mince pies, with a cheery, 'There you are, mother, Happy Christmas'. They knew that 'Mother' would be a regular customer all next year as a result, so it was a worthwhile gesture.

The buses and trams were filled with happy shoppers, crowded against each other with their bags. Happy because they had had a Christmas experience, and because they were not worrying already how they were going to pay for it. They had saved from their housekeeping budgets for weeks for this holiday, put money away into Christmas Clubs which were run by a wide variety of shops. The money was there, already allocated, to spend, and spend it they had, with all the joy of spending a windfall!

By the time the Christmas tea was on the table, and the children were all playing with their presents, the older ones sitting reminiscing or listening to the radio, everyone was calmly happy. It had been yet another good Christmas and one looked forward to the next. No one worried about the debts incurred, and the shops still had their decorations up, for those who ventured into town to see them right up to New Year's Day, when the January sales began. But that is another tale!

SEASONAL CELEBRATIONS

Christmas with the American Presidents

In 1997 the one hundred and ninety-sixth Christmas was celebrated at the White House, beginning with John Adams and now the present incumbents, the Clintons. What stories the old walls could tell if they could speak! Diary entries, letters and biographies have all recorded some of these seasonal events, and below is a tantalizing glimpse of just some. The bibliography for these few runs to dozens of books and papers.

Accounts of George Washington's Christmases are scanty. George Washington spent Christmas night in 1776 crossing the Delaware River in dreadful conditions. This event, covered in hundreds of poems and stories, was heroic rather than nostalgic. Christmas in 1777 was little better – at Valley Forge, Washington and his men had a miserable Christmas dinner of fowl cooked in a broth of turnips, cabbage and potatoes. But in 1783 he retired and spent Christmas at Mount Vernon with his family and there were 'rousing cheers, song, pistol shots and firecrackers'. His retirement initiated a new Christmas pastime in Washington – long before the custom of sending Christmas cards was to become popular, the retired President would spend his time writing Christmas letters.

A relation who spent that Christmas with the Washingtons wrote this account:

I must tell you what a charming day I spent at Mt. Vernon with Mama and Sally. The General and Madame came home on Christmas Eve and such a racket as the servants made. They were glad of their coming. Three handsome young officers came with them. All Christmas afternoon people came to pay their respects and duty. Among these were stately dames and gay young women. The General seemed happy and Mrs Washington was up before daybreak making everything as agreeable as possible.

That was the last account of Christmas from Mount Vernon. John Adams took his place at 1600 Pennsylvania Avenue, which was called 'The President's House' at that time and only became known as the White House later. President Adams went on record as being the first president to hold a children's party at the residence. This was for his young granddaughter, Suzannah, and it appears from records that there were as many mishaps as at any children's party! One child broke a dish belonging to Suzannah, who in return bit off the nose of the new wax doll which had been the Christmas-tree present for her little guest!

A happier scene was recorded during the Christmas of 1805, when Thomas Jefferson celebrated a Christmas party with his six grandchildren. To a party of a hundred guests the President played a merry jig on his fiddle.

In fact some of the merriest stories of the presidential Christmases are those which mention children or grandchildren. President Jackson, 1829–37, is said to have enjoyed snowball fights with his little guests from a local orphanage. Jackson's wife had died early, and he shared his residence with relatives. One day his nephew asked, 'Did you ever hear of a Christmas without presents, Uncle Andrew?' and the great man replied, 'Yes, once there was a little boy who never had a toy, and when his mother died he was all alone in the world. I was that boy.' As a result of this he made sure that there were plenty of presents, both practical and frivolous, under the tree for the children he had in his home.

There have been many other children's parties: Theodore Roosevelt's wife issued invitations to some six hundred children to a party where adults and nurses were not admitted except to attend to the most timid of children, who feasted on creamed oysters among other things; Herbert C. Hoover and his family gave their first presidential Christmas party at the White House in 1929 and it included carol singing by candlelight around the big dark house. Their second Christmas in office was quite different because of the Depression after the Wall Street Crash, and everywhere conditions were bad. Christmas would not come to many homes in 1930, so the First Lady decided to hold a special party. She sent out a most unusual invitation which read as follows:

Mrs. Hoover
and
Peggy, Ann and Peter
request the pleasure of the company of

on Wednesday, December twenty-third
from half after three to five o'clock

THE WHITE HOUSE
WASHINGTON

This is not like the Christmas parties you usually go to, where you get lots of toys and presents to take home, and very good things to eat.

But it is a party where you bring toys and warm gay sweaters or candy, or things other children would like who otherwise would not have much Christmas.

For Santa Claus has sent word that he is not going to be able, by himself, to take care of all the little boys and girls he wants to this year, and he has asked other people to help him as much as possible.

So if you bring some presents with you, we will send them all to him to distribute. And we will send most of the candy and 'snappers' and cake and 'such' to him too!

The party was a great success and the lack of real gifts was made up for by the entertainments – the band of the US Marines played Christmas tunes, there was storytelling and every child had small favours, usually noisy ones such as tooters etc!

In 1981 the Reagans held a Christmas party for children with impaired hearing. The entertainment was provided by two members of the Osmonds, who themselves had hearing difficulties, and Mrs Reagan even learnt some simple phrases in sign language. The President's speech that year focused heavily on children; he said, 'Christmas means so much because of one special child. But Christmas also reminds us that all children are special, that they are gifts from God, gifts beyond price that mean more than any presents that money can buy. In their love and laughter, in our hopes for their future, lies the true meaning of Christmas.'

Not all White House Christmases have been for children of course and there are many accounts of elegant balls and fine dinners, such as the one described by the local reporter writing about a party held by the President and Mrs Polk in 1847.

> On entering I found a comfortable room full, with President Polk standing before the fire bowing and shaking hands.
>
> The First Lady of the Land was seated on the sofa, engaged with some half a dozen ladies in lively conversation; and though ill and clumsy in millinery, yet I will try to describe what she had on. A Maroon-coloured velvet dress, with short sleeves, trimmed with very deep lace, and a handsome pink headdress was all that struck the eye of the general observer.

The most unusual party, especially for its time, was that given by President Buchanan, who was without the company of a First Lady, and considered a 'lonely man'. In 1857 he gave a party for thirty American Indians from the tribes of the Poncas, Pawnees and Pottowatomies. A report of the day stated that while the Pottowatomies arrived in 'citizen's dress', the Pawnees and Poncas 'were in their grandest attire, and more than profuse of paint and feathers'.

The Nation's Christmas Tree

The largest and most ancient of the grand Sequoias in the General Grant National Park is dedicated to the famous general. Sequoia trees are the oldest living things in the world and this antediluvian monument was already mature at the time of Christ's birth. Since 1925 it has been the site of a special Christmas ceremony and the tree is known as the Nation's Christmas Tree.

The most recent account of a Presidential Christmas describes the 1997 White House theme, which was based on Christmas as seen through the eyes of a child. The description of the traditional gingerbread house set up in the State Dining Room sums up this theme without further comment!

The traditional Gingerbread House . . . depicts a Santa's Victorian home complete with his workshop, reindeer stables, and Santa with his sleigh preparing for departure from his rooftop. Within his workshop, you can see Santa's Elves busy at work surrounded by toys made of candy, marzipan and chocolate. Socks can be seen in Santa's sleigh, preparing to help him with the busy night ahead. The gingerbread house consists of 80 pounds of gingerbread, 40 pounds of chocolate and 10 pounds of marzipan, and is entirely edible. The White House pastry chefs created this delicious and fanciful masterpiece.

Old Japan and the Samurai Santa

Mariko Okawa of the Felissimo Christmas Museum, Hakodate, Japan; translated by Akio Onishi

A request to one of Japan's best Christmas historians uncovered the following fascinating account of a Christmas unknown to Westerners – and to most Japanese too. It includes an amusing account of Santa dressed as a Samurai.

Francis Xavier was from Portugal in 1549 and taught us Christianity about 400 years ago. It was the first experience of this for the Japanese and Christmas became popular throughout Japan from that time. The first recorded Christmas Mass was celebrated at Yamaguchi Church in 1552. Even today there are *Kakure* (secret Christians), who hide that they are

Christians, and they still use Latin when they sing Christmas carols. This style of celebrating Christmas has not changed since the custom began 400 years ago.

In 1639 National Isolation was imposed upon Japan, and most Christians changed their religion at that time, but some, especially the *Kakure*, kept Christmas in secret all through the persecution.

In 1854, American Navy Commodore Perry opened National Isolation and Japan began to take to Western culture like a dry sponge to water.

But Christmas was not well known at that time. In 1875 in Harajo School in the Ginza area of Tokyo, Christmas was celebrated. It was strange and amusing because Santa Claus appeared dressed like a Samurai.

In Taisho period (1912–26) a lot of Western countries began ordering Christmas decorations and toys from Japan instead of from Germany. Japanese manufacturers made Christmas lights for the tree, and dolls of Santa Claus for ornamentation; some were made of celluloid. And aluminium artificial Christmas trees came from Japan also. These Christmas things were getting pretty common and easy to find in Western department stores and toy shops after the Second World War.

A lot of beautiful Christmas customs had come to Japan from America, and in return occupied Japan was exporting Christmas decorations, toys and china. During that time Japan was like Santa Claus' Toyland Factory. This continued until Hong Kong and Taiwan became famous for exporting goods.

Of course Japan was getting used to Christmas and Christmas customs and Christmas lifestyle and it was like the original, early Christian Japanese Christmas, though no longer celebrated by all Japanese as a Christian celebration. For example, sometimes for Christmas dinner it was popular for each family to cook Hamburgers and Stew, following the example of American style cooking from after the war. By the way, Japanese Christmas cake was a new experience for the Japanese, and they used to buy buttercream sponge cakes from the shops which served Western people. Until today, the buttercream or fresh cream cake has been the popular Japanese Christmas cake.

Japanese had fast growth economy from 1950 to 1960. By now Japanese people were buying lots of Christmas presents, and had parties, and cooked Christmas dinner for their children. After a while these children grew up and they talked about their nice memories of Christmas to their children. Thus Christmas was handed down from generation to generation. Recently

Christmas illumination is becoming more beautiful and more popular year by year.

Now there is hardly a family which does not celebrate Christmas Western style, like American, English, French, German, Scandinavian and so on, which means that Japanese Christmas style is fading out. But it only has real meaning for a few people in Japan. We hope Japanese style Christmas will be popular again some day.

Christmas as a Child in Germany

Ciaran Reynolds

If Bethlehem is the nucleus from which all Christmas religious celebration and belief stems, so Germany has been the heartland of the traditions of Christmas as we know them. From here comes the Christmas Tree, the glass bauble, the Advent calendar and the Christmas-card industry. Here too the people celebrate somehow the commercial aspects of Christmas without losing the essential Christmas spirit. The German Christmas markets are renowned and copied all over the world. The German academic world has done more for the serious study of the different aspects of Christmas than any other country; even in America, which is very close behind Germany in this respect, there is not the spectrum of subject matter which one can find in a German library. First is an account of a childhood Christmas set in 1934.

It was 1934. I was staying in a little village called Königstein a few miles from Frankfurt-am-Main, among beautiful surroundings of tree-studded countryside, and literally just the place for a Christmas in the snow.

The family I was staying with consisted of ten, when all were assembled together for the festive season. The elderly parents, three sons and their wives and two grandchildren.

Christmas started with a visit to Frankfurt, then a beautiful old city, where an annual evening fête took place (Christmas market) in the market square. Here with the enormous traditional Christmas Tree as a centre piece, the square was thronged with warmly clad, happy people, some singing carols, others holding torch lights of flame, and intermingling among the crowd were smartly clad German officers, rattling tins of money, collecting towards the Winter Help Fund. Officers laughed and joked with everyone.

A hot-chestnut man was busy selling steaming nuts, there was music from a barrel organ and a cheeky monkey jumping about on the top. People were dancing around the tree, so it was, indeed, a seasonal joy for all men.

Our personal Christmas commenced on the Eve, when during that evening, about four o'clock, one of the three living rooms was prepared by Frau Mettenheimer. About six o'clock we were all summoned together. The door was then opened to a seemingly dark room, curtains drawn against the snowy evening – and what a delight met our eyes!

All around the room stood miniature fir trees, each on its own table, sparkling with coloured lights and small glass baubles. A lighted candle stood near each tree. The magic of that room, with its truly personal appeal to each individual, has never left me.

Each tree was surrounded with a few tiny wrapped gifts, and soon the floor was strewn with festive paper and ribbon. Everyone seemed to be kissing each other with thanks, and the adults were toasting one another in ruby red wine, while we younger ones enjoyed less intoxicating drinks.

Following our evening meal, we all donned overcoats, ear-hugging hats, warm gloves and scarves, and drove in the cars to the small village cemetery among the beautiful pine trees and surrounding woods. It was a great surprise to me to see each grave adorned with a little fir tree. Some had been decorated, flowers had been put at each grave, and every one had a candle burning as a watchlight. This was an enchanting spectacle.

Christmas Day was celebrated in very much the same way as I had known in England. Present opening, a great deal of eating, on a more massive scale than at home. The adults playing bridge and smoking and drinking Schnapps. We others went in a car to the top of a small mountain, walked off our meal and admired the view. It was a quiet family day, as was

The Rhineland giftbringer of long ago – Frau Berchta brings her gifts.

Boxing Day, but I shall never forget the unique customs of that small village. While the snow lightly fell and settled upon the fir trees, it looked like fairyland. Even the cemetery had a fairytale atmosphere, as the warmth from the candles melted the snow around, and the flakes settled upon the little fir trees.

La Bûche, la Galette et l'Allégresse!

CHRISTMAS IN PROVENCE

Frédéric Mistral

Provence has customs all of its own, distinct from those in the rest of France. One of the most enduring is the Santons, small figures which are made for the Nativity scenes. These include the woodseller, the butcher, baker and candlestick maker – in fact all the tradespeople one can imagine in a rural economy. The following account of a nineteenth-century Christmas paints a wonderful picture of Christmas in the farmhouse of the author Frédéric Mistral's childhood home.

For my Father, who was faithful to ancient custom, the feast of the year was Christmas Eve. That day the farm labourers finished their work early, and off they would go with gifts from my mother wrapped in a napkin – a great *galette l'huile*, a roll of nougat, a cluster of dried figs, a sheep's milk cheese from our own sheep, a salad of celery and a bottle of matured wine. Off the peasants would go to 'place the log' in their own homes. Those who stayed at the farm were those with no home to go to, or sometimes a relative, who was perhaps an old bachelor, would arrive at night saying, 'Merry Christmas! I've come to place the log with all of you.'

Then all together we would go joyously to find the Christmas log, which according to strict tradition, had to be from a fruit tree. We heaved it back to the farm, one after the other, with the eldest at one end and the youngest at the rear. Three times we would drag it around the kitchen, and then we arrived in front of the hearth, my father would pour a glass of mature wine solemnly over the log saying,

> *Allégresse! Allégresse!*
> *Mes beaux enfants,*
> *Que Dieu nous comble d'allégresse!*

Avec Noël tout bien vient!
Dieu nous fasse la grâce de voir l'année prochaine,
Et, sinon plus nombreux, puissions-nous n'y pas être moins!

Happiness!
My fine children,
May God fill us all with happiness!
With Christmas comes all good things good!
May God grant that we see the next year through,
And even if there are not more of us, let there not be fewer!

And crying together, 'Happiness, Happiness, Happiness', we placed the log on the hearth, and as the first flame licked from it, my father would cross himself and recite '*À la Bûche, Boute feu*!', 'To the Log, at the heart of the fire!' Then we would all have supper.

Putting the Christmas log in the grate. A nineteenth-century Provençal drawing.

Oh, the holy table! Holy in truth with all the family round it, at peace and happy. Instead of the lamp which hung all the year we had three tall candles burning on the table, and if a wick bent towards anyone, it was bad luck. At either end of the table there was a plate of green corn in water, to sprout for the Feast of Saint Barbara. On the three white cloths there appeared the blessed dishes, snails, which everyone picked from the shells with a long nail; fried cod and mullet with olives; shrimps; celery with a dressing of pepper and vinegar; and these were followed by a pile of dainty sweetmeats reserved for this feast, flat cakes made with olive oil, raisins, almonds, nougat, paradise apples, and most important the great Christmas loaf, quartered crosswise, which must not be taken until the first quarter had been given to the first poor person who came begging.

A Canadian Christmas Mosaic

Unlike the American Christmas, which is something of a melting pot of Christmas customs, many Canadian immigrant groups retain the customs from their countries of origin. Thus Canada boasts a colourful mosaic of many distinct customs. To quote Louise Quildon, who wrote about such customs in her book, *Canadian Christmas*, 'Christmas is a time rich in meaning and in memories. It is a time they (immigrants) recall the close family ties, the feasting, the fun and above all, the colourful ceremony of a time past.' It is little wonder then, that many immigrant groups attempt to preserve the customs associated with the celebration of Christmas. . . . Among several of the groups studied, it was shown that some traditional customs had to be adapted and others still abandoned entirely as not suited to the urban Canadian environment. However, looking back nostalgically at a gentler time of our parents and grandparents, here are a few observations of Canadian Christmas.

Armenian Christians fared better in Canada than back home, where, when it was in the hands of the USSR, they found it impossible to observe Christmas at all. Being orthodox, they celebrate Christmas on 6 January, when the boy carol singers collected foodstuffs at the houses, which were taken to the church for a

Canadian Indian crèche scene with buffalo, bear and fox, the wise men represented by the chieftains of the woods, plains and Inuit Indian nations.

huge breakfast for everyone to eat after the Christmas service.

The Czechs, the Slovaks and the Dutch still have a visit from St Nicholas on 6 December. Christmas is a time to end quarrels and apologize for wrongs done among the Canadian Czechoslovaks, while the Germans observe all the elements which they have lent to the Western world, and of these perhaps the tree is most important to them. This has a *Rauschgold-engel* on its top, a traditional angel made originally from gilded tinfoil. They have spicy gingerbread and cookies of all kinds and Christmas dinner is often goose.

Poles, Hungarians, Ukraines, Italians – all the traditions from their home countries exist side by side with new traditions adapted to suit the Canadian lifestyle, and their customs are to be found elsewhere in this book under their countries of origin. Canada is a new country with old values, and this is a fact they are proud of.

Fun 'neath a Nigerian Sun

Miss A.E. Allen

An account from a missionary teacher who went to Toro in Nigeria at the very end of the nineteenth century.

To begin with, Christmas in Toro is unlike Christmas at home.

Can you fancy Christmas without holly, without church bells, crackers, parties and shopping etc? I must not add without plum puddings, for some of us do get them sent out from the Army and Navy Stores. We do have

A Christmas bullock, Toro, Central Africa.

beef, in huge quantities. Two Christmas bullocks are killed at this station (Kabarole) on Christmas Eve, a very solemn preparation. It was carried into the house piled up in large native baskets, a 'Baron' having been reserved for our own Christmas meal, the rest reserved for the teachers' feast, when about 150 men and women teachers came from all the surrounding stations, some walking over 50 miles.

In England, Christmas is essentially the children's 'good time', but so far this is not the case in this part of Africa. The King and chiefs give big feasts to their underlings. The guests sit in groups of ten or twelve round a huge flat native basket filled with steaming plantains neatly wrapped in banana leaves; at one side stand two other baskets, one containing chunks of boiled meat, the other salted gravy on a leaf. First the attendant comes round and pours water over the hands of all the guests, who proceed to knead the plantains into little cups, which they dip into the gravy and eat, sometimes offering them to their friends.

I suppose you know that all the days in the tropics are the same length, so that Christmas Day is quite as long as Midsummer's Day. No drawing round the Yule log and roasting chestnuts. The sun rises at 6 a.m., and Morning Service is crammed from rail to rail, and there are no decorations in Church lest the people here should misunderstand and associate it with their ancient spiritworship. At 4 o'clock, we Europeans meet for tea and tennis, and end up with a dinner of Roast Beef and Plum Pudding.

On Boxing Day, the Natives have racing and jumping games, kings, chiefs and some thousand spectators. But the race of men with children on their backs was, I think, not so amusing for the young burdens as it was for the spectators.

I'm Dreaming of a Maltese Christmas

Frank L. Scicluna

You are not likely to have a white Christmas in Malta. Weather conditions resemble those of Bethlehem, the birthplace of Christ. The temperature during Yuletide fluctuates from a maximum of 19°C to a minimum of 9°C.

There are certain characteristics that make Maltese Christmas different from that of many other countries. The streets of towns and villages are decorated and lit with multicoloured lights called *Festuni*. Shop windows display the usual Christmas decorations and a large variety of toys and presents to lure Christmas shoppers who jam the streets. Christmas trees, *is-sigra tal-Milied*, and the figure of Father Christmas – Santa Claus – are seen all over the place. The main feature, which is a typically Maltese tradition, is the number of cribs, *presepji*, that can be seen in public places and in private homes.

The first Maltese crib we know of is that found at the convent of the Benedictine Nuns in Mdina. . . . Traditionally, the crib figures, *pasturi*, are made of clay. Apart from the principal figures they include shepherds minding their flocks, street singers, the shepherd's pipe and drum players, a farmer feeding his animals, a woman carrying a flour sack, the sleeping man and the man sprawling on his stomach perched on top of the grotto to look down on the Baby Jesus. These fragile clay figures were easily acquired a few years ago. Now modern plastic figures are more commonly found in the Maltese family crib.

Nearly in every town and village a procession is held with children carrying a small statue of Baby Jesus and singing Christmas carols along the way. In every parish church in Malta and Gozo during midnight mass, a small child, dressed in a white alb, recites a sermon narrating the birth of Christ.

Christmas offers a splendid occasion for family gatherings. In most houses an attractively decorated Christmas tree is put up, beneath which are placed the various presents wrapped in colourful paper. Christmas pudding, *il-pudinatal-Milied*, and turkey, *id-dundjan*, became popular during the First and Second World Wars when thousands of sailors and soldiers from the British Empire were stationed in Malta. The Island was a military and naval base for the Allies. Prior to this, the rooster, *Serduq*, rather than the turkey, was the bird to be served at Christmas dinner. The traditional Christmas banquet normally includes the delicious Maltese dish called *Timpana*, baked macaroni covered with crusty pastry. A special kind of honey and treacle rings, *qaghaq talghasel*, are eaten during the Christmas festivities.

An old tradition that survives up to this day is the sowing of wheat, grain and canary seed on clots of cotton in flat pans four weeks before Christmas and nurtured in the darkness of cupboards in the kitchen. These seeds shoot up and remain as white as Santa's beard. They are then placed next to the infant Jesus in the crib.

A custom which unfortunately vanished many years ago was the playing of bagpipes, *iz-zaqq*. They characterized the music of the shepherds who tended their flocks on Christmas night. Folk memory in Gozo records that for the midnight mass on Christmas Eve bagpipes were played in churches, striking a genuine pastoral note.

A Magnificent Danish Christmas!

Marie Louise Paludan

Hans Christian Andersen is recorded as having said of the full Danish Christmas that it is 'Magnificent, quite unforgettably magnificent'.

A Danish Christmas is like a piece of music. Depending on inclination, tradition and means, you can play it simply as a solo flute – or build it up bit by bit into a crashing orchestral piece. The melody is the same. But if you decide to celebrate a Danish Christmas with all the trimmings, you face a formidable task. It takes time and hard work but the finished result brings incomparable rewards.

Well-organized people have Christmas in mind all the year round. They buy their Christmas gifts when they come across the right thing and slip them secretly into a special drawer.

Christmas preparations begin proper with greetings cards and letters for abroad. Letters have to be written in October and gifts wrapped in Christmas paper with stars and hearts and red tape, and dispatched two months before Christmas. And as you stamp your mail the Christmas feeling is strengthened yet again by the sight of the Christmas seal of the year. Each year a new design of seal is issued – a mini work of art. One of the most beautiful was the set of seals designed one year by Queen Margarethe: a sheet of music-making angels (in 1970). The revenue from the Christmas seals goes towards convalescence facilities for ailing children.

One of many customs, the Advent wreath made from scented pine with four candles, one for each week, begins the Christmas countdown. Danish families also hang up a sheaf of corn for the birds, up in an apple tree or on a balcony, and it is often the children who hang the pinecone decoration on the front door.

Christmas Eve is the biggest evening of the year, and the most beautiful, and the day preceding the busiest! Last-minute shopping, putting up the

A Danish family dance around the Christmas tree before the gift-giving ceremony, c. 1970.
Danish Foreign Ministry.

tree, impatient children sent to the shops to buy their own personal decorations. Dad has almost certainly forgotten one or two purchases, and removes himself discreetly for a couple of hours. And all the while someone is climbing up and down a ladder, or there is a hustle and bustle behind closed doors while the tree is decorated, and a wonderful smell of something cooking wafts from the kitchen. The table has to be laid – with a special Christmas cloth or centrepiece, and everything has to be arranged in time so that those members of the family wishing to go to the Christmas Service may do so.

The traditional Christmas Eve meal starts with rice pudding containing a solitary almond. The finder wins a prize, often a marzipan pig. The menu then moves on to roast pork, goose, duck or turkey. Duck stuffed with

A nineteenth-century Danish Christmas card.

apples and prunes served with candied potatoes, red cabbage and jelly has a long tradition behind it.

The tree is hidden behind closed doors, and after supper all the candles are lit, with a bucket of water close by! The supper over, the doors are opened. This is the climax of Christmas. Now peace can descend. We have time to inspect the tree and its tinsel, the hearts, angels, cones, flags, fairies and stars. There are birds and squirrels made out of fircones, tiny ships out of walnut shells, delicate and delightful objects in straw, glass and paper, turning and sparkling.

We form a ring round the tree, holding hands, singing all the Christmas carols we can remember. Perhaps someone reads a verse or two from the Bible – then the moment arrives when we open the parcels under the tree. Wrapping gifts up in an attractive manner with beautiful paper is an art the children and young folk enjoy dearly. Surprise is an important element.

Christmas Day for most Danes is a boisterous sociable day; it means a groaning lunch table and much of the food is home-made. One evening before New Year, we burn all the remaining candle ends right down – with idle bets on which will last longest.

So Christmas is over – Well, not quite. It lasts thirteen days. The twelfth is Twelfth Night. The Danes light three candles as a token substitute for the Christmas Tree which has now been moved to the garden and decorated with strings of fat and nuts for the birds.

Wigilia

POLISH CUSTOMS

Monica Gardner

*Despite being for so long under Communist rule, Poland has always
maintained its Christmas intact. Traditional Christmas Eve suppers, the
uniquely Polish Krakow crib competition and a host of wonderful
Christmas songs and carols have stayed alive in this tormented country.
The following account from 1917 details some of the chief elements of
the Polish Christmas, which have changed little over the ensuing decades.*

There are few countries so rich in national customs as Poland. They are
clung to in the peasants' cottages, carried out in the homes of the rich, kept
up fondly by the exiles far away from home. Most beautiful among them is the
festival of Christmas Eve. On that night a feast is held which is not only a
sacred family gathering, but has its own sweet and solemn religious meaning.

Deep snow lies on the ground. The cold is intense, dry and frosty. There is
the gay sound of tinkling bells as the guests, muffled in furs, drive up in
sledges, little bells ringing on the horses' heads. All is ready for the supper;
but it must not begin till the first star appears in the sky, which in Poland
would be about 6 o'clock. Therefore this Christmas supper, besides the
name by which it is generally known, 'Wigilia', the Vigil – is known also as
the Star supper. The children are watching eagerly for the star to rise. When
at last it twinkles in the sky, the signal is given, and all go in to supper.

The dining room is lit with unusual brilliance. In memory of our Saviour's
birth in a manger, straw or hay is laid upon the table under a white cloth.
Before the company seat themselves, the father, or head of the family, takes
a plate containing a wafer. It has been specially prepared and blessed by the
parish priest and has some sacred sign stamped upon it – IHS, or a picture
of the Nativity, with perhaps a border of flowers. The father makes a little
speech bidding those present to be at peace with God. He then breaks the
wafer with the mother, and then with everyone present. The absent ones are
not forgotten. Where we send Christmas cards, Poles send these blessed

wafers first tearing off a small corner to show those who are to receive them that the donor has broken it with them as a token of affection. How many Polish families have been parted from each other by exile! We can guess at the tender pleasure they feel when across the sea come these little white wafers to remind them of the old times when they too sat round the straw-covered table, to prove to them that though their place is now empty, they are there in spirit and remembered with love.

After the wafer is broken, during which ceremony everyone wishes each other a happy Christmas and the beautiful Polish carols are sung, the supper is eaten. It is the first meal of the day, as Christmas Eve is a strict fast in Poland. There are generally about eleven courses, but they may not include any meat. Almond soup, consisting of almonds, raisins, rice and milk, must always be served; and beetroot soup is also often on the table. Then come different kinds of fish – baked pike, for instance, or carp; vegetable dishes, very curious to our notions, such as small bags of pastry, filled with sauerkraut and swimming in butter, and cabbage leaves wrapped around fried or boiled millet.

'Polish Christmas'. This old Polish print shows starboys, the Christmas Eve feast with carp, the tree and the Nativity.

The sweets include Polish poppyseed cakes, greatly beloved by the Polish children. They are a compound of white poppyseeds and jam in alternate layers. These are followed by elaborate ginger cakes and all kinds of pastry. The dessert is such as we have in England in midwinter – apples, oranges, nuts and dried fruits. Hungarian wine and the famous old Polish national drink of mead are served with the solid foods.

Towards the end of the supper, it is obvious that something special is going to happen. The children are all led away from the dining room into another apartment. In comes a person dressed as Father Christmas, but who in Poland is called the 'Starman'. (He is traditionally accompanied by the Starboys, who carry a lighted star lantern and sing carols.) Very often he is the parish priest in disguise. He examines the children in their catechism, and reproves those who answer wrong, and sometimes, in extreme cases, arranged beforehand with the parents, has recourse to a little birch!

Presently at the sign from the mother, the Starman tells the children that he has brought them rewards for their good conduct, from his own country, Starland, and his helpers have been arranging them in the dining room. He leads the eager children back to the dining room, where a transformation scene has taken place. Fancy lanterns and lights of all descriptions illuminate the room. Beautifully decked Christmas trees adorn the corners; and we can guess the rest of the scene, because children are the same all over the world.

After supper all the family, with the servants, gather around the fireplace. They sing Christmas hymns. Then up come young boys from the village, carrying a great paper star lantern, singing carols. They are given presents and, the children safely packed off to bed, the elders spend the evening chatting till midnight. Then they drive in sledges through the deep snow to midnight mass.

The village church, lights streaming from its windows on to the frozen white ground outside, is crowded with the peasants in their heavy sheepskins, and topboots; with their sonorous voices chanting the Christmas hymns. They too have broken the Christmas wafer. What Pole has not? Even the cattle are not left out. Their wafer is crumbled into their food in memory of Christ being laid in a manger.

Christmas Day itself is kept like an ordinary Sunday. But there are several more little traditions connected with Christmastide. During the days around Christmas, beginning with Christmas Eve, Starboys carolling the Christmas songs go from house to house carrying the *Szopka*, a miniature shed with puppets that act wonderfully well the sacred story of Christmas. Two days

The Star Children Choir of expatriate Polish children at St Mary of the Angels Benedictine Priory Church, Cardiff, 1982.

after Christmas, on St John the Evangelist's Day, the congregation goes up to the altar rails. The priest comes to each one and gives him or her the sacred chalice to drink from. This is in memory of St John's martyrdom in boiling oil.

Then comes Twelfth Night, the Epiphany. The people take with them to church small jewellery boxes, containing a gold ring, some incense, and amber in memory of the gifts of the Magi, and chalk. These objects are blessed; and when the owners return home, they draw with the chalk on every door in the house the initials K.M.B. with a cross after each. These letters stand for the names of the Three Kings, which according to tradition were Kaspar, Melchior and Balthasar; and they remain on the doors all year.

As we have seen, Christmas carols are a great feature of a Polish Christmas. They have been handed down for centuries, and are extremely beautiful. (The Polish National Hymn is a carol entitled 'God is Born'.) A Pole who escaped from Siberia has told a touching story about these Christmas carols. He was languishing in his dungeon. All alone as he was he had lost count of time. Suddenly one night he heard among the clanking fetters a burst of the well-known Polish carol rising from the cell next to his. Then for the first time he knew that Poles were near him and it was Christmas Eve.

Russia's Three Christmases

Various contributors

Russia has claim to three Christmases: pre-Revolution, Soviet and post-Soviet. Pre-Revolution was half Orthodox and half pre-Christian Kalends; Soviet was a commercial pageant; post-Soviet strives to regain its pre-Revolution roots, with the restrictions of the new state. The following contributions cover more nostalgic elements of the romantic tsarist Christmas as told by English servants working for the Russian noble families in the early years of the twentieth century.

Christmas in Tsarist Russia

The first account is from Mr Thompson, a gardener from Yorkshire. He was a near neighbour of my family. He was brought up in a Russian household as the son of the head gardener there before the First World War. This account is pieced together from the story which he told to me in 1957 when he was in his seventies. He lived in Russia until he was about twenty years old.

A traditional Russian Christmas card from the pre-Soviet era, c. 1890.

The thing I remember most as a small boy, son of a gardener in a stately household near St Petersburg, is the Christmas tree, oh and the food. So much and to me so different.

All the staff were invited to a huge party held for the villagers and people round about. It was held in this big ballroom place, with chandeliers with hundreds of candles. All the gold-painted scrollwork on the walls and doors glinted in the light of them, and the tree was right in the middle. That too was covered in lit candles, and liveried flunkies hovered around with snuffers on long sticks in case there was a dripping candle.

The tree had mostly edible decorations on it, sugar plums my mother called them, though they were not all plums and then those that were tended to be stuffed with a sort of chocolate paste or a stiff fruit paste called *mermalade*, rather than being sugared! There were small rosy apples, nuts which had been gilded and hung on strings, shaped biscuits and *pryaniki*, which were small iced honeycakes.

The tinsel had been draped in such a way that the whole tree looked like the top of the pies my mother made, latticed to save pastry she used to say, all criss-crossed. All the presents were on two long tables either side of the tree, and were handed out by footmen. Those wrapped in green and blue paper were for the men and boys, and on the other side, pink and yellow paper for the women and girls.

The presents were useful things like warm shawls or aprons or heavy stockings for the women, and gloves or even boots for the men. The children had toys of course. My father, who had worked on the estate for over ten years, got a silver watch and chain one year, much to the envy of his under-gardeners. Working in such winter temperatures as they had, he deserved it. He had lost two fingers with frostbite.

After the presents we played games for a while which gave the household a chance to have a brief conversation with each villager and member of staff, then we went back to our homes. One year when I was twelve, my father took me to the village where a group of men and boys met at the home of the village elder. There we sang *kolyadki*, old Christmas songs. Of course some carols too. The *kolyadki* were not liked by the priests

A traditional Russian Christmas card from the pre-Soviet era, c. 1890.

because they originated in pagan times. We came back to Britain in 1906 because my grandmother needed looking after when my grandfather died. I think we had the best of it, things began to go downhill soon after that. A friend from schooldays in Russia used to write to me about the events. But his letters stopped in 1915. Never heard from him again.

The next account comes from an old lady who was in her eighties when this interview was conducted in 1980. She gave her name as 'Alice will do'! In 1910 she went as a junior governess to an 'important' family in Moscow.

I remember being very impressed by the beautiful church services. The churches were covered wall to wall with lovely pictures of saints' 'Icons'. Some decorated with gold or silver or even precious stones. It was very tiring as the service was so long, about three hours I think! There were no seats like in an English church – you had to stand. But the chanting and singing was like listening to heavenly choirs! I was a junior governess, little better than a nurserymaid really, and treated like one of the children by the upper governess! She was so strict. It was very fashionable to have an English governess for the children of the big families in those days. I think some of the other houses also had a French teacher living in, as French was the fashionable language to speak.

The Master's brother was a priest. I was quite alarmed by him actually. He was so big – I was only 4'11" tall – with a long bushy black beard. He seemed to disapprove of everything as far as I could understand. The worst thing was that he spent Christmases with us. The children of the house disliked him as much as I did, I think. There was a Christmas tree, huge, decorated with candles. There was plenty of lovely food. We 'servants' always had our own Christmas dinner with several baked pike served with a sort of stewed apple

A sleigh-ride in Moscow, c. 1870.

done in batter and fried in butter. There were little patties made from gamebirds of all kinds – left over from the dining room of course, but a typical treat none the less, and a soup made from fish called *ooha*. Dessert was small jellied sweetmeats – *pastilla* – with a white foamy top, a bit like marshmallow, but tasting of pure fruit. These would be served on trays with another Russian speciality called *mermalade*, which were squares of stiff fruit jellies, rather like the old English and Spanish fruit cheeses. And of course there were several *Tortes* – rich layer cakes with preserves, nuts, fruits and sugar – which were served with tea from a great samovar.

We ate at about six o'clock – because the domestic servants were serving the traditional dinner to the house and guests between three and five o'clock, which was always the traditional Russian dinner time.

Some of us would then go to spend part of the evening with acquaintances from other houses, and enjoy some singing and games. The 'priest-uncle' frowned upon such 'heathen practices'.

With the Reindeer Herders in Lapland

Maria Hubert, Bryan Foster and others

The Lapp Christmas is different to others because it is not the most important festival in the year. Easter is the most significant, followed in some parts by the Feast of the Annunciation, and other places set great store by Twelfth Night. Some have their main festival at different times of the year and while Christmas is a recognized holiday, both religious and secular, there is no one special festival other than Easter in pre-Christian times. However, there were special rites, costumes and foods which were associated with the end of year around Christmas time.

Most of the winter they follow the reindeer herds, and many Lapps are still nomadic.

The legend has it that the Old Man of the Snows drives the reindeer down from the mountains ahead of the snow. This character became, somehow, the Giftbringer (he brought the snow which warmed the earth, and the deer which was the lifeline of the early Lapps). He is *Youlo-puki*, or the 'Yule elf', from which character many of the characteristics attributed to Santa Claus were derived.

There is an old seventeenth-century story relating to Christmas and the Lapps. There was a group of Christian Lapps who were really not very good Christians, leaning more to their heathen practices. They would not go to church, even on Christmas Day. Instead a sacrifice was made to the *Youlo-herrer* ('Yuletide people'), who were supposed to be able to fly around the skies at Christmas time. This belief actually has roots in the Wild Hordes and other legendary spirits which Northern people believed to be the souls of the dead. It was considered important to keep on the good side of these spirits, to maintain peace.

Anyway, the food from each family which would have been eaten (except at the time of the statutory Christmas-Eve fast) was collected, put into a basket on to which warmed fat was poured to make a sort of fat cake with lots of goodies inside. On Christmas morning this basket of fat cake was hoisted up to the tallest tree, so that the Yuletide people could have their Christmas party. (In Sweden, food is put out for the *Tomten*, Christmas elves, so that they will enjoy Christmas, and not annoy the householder with their naughty tricks!) On old divining drums there appear representations in pictures of the Yuleboat sacrifice, showing the story is based on very ancient custom.

A Welsh Holly Tree

Eirwen Jones

Christmas in Wales, despite the Chapel upbringing of most people, was a joyous, even merry affair by and large. There were many ancient customs observed right up to the 1950s; the cock crow service (Plygain), for example, which is a remnant of the pre-Reformation night service. The

The visit of the Mari Lwyd in early twentieth-century Wales. Courtesy of the Museum of Welsh Life.

women stayed home and made 'Taffy' and cakes to see who would marry first. The men went to the chapels and sang a most haunting polyphony. Nowadays, where Plygain remains, women join in. The 'Mari Lwyd', consisting of a horse's skull covered with a sheet and decorated with ribbons, was carried round the houses by an entourage of men who would sing a rhyming 'battle' with the householders, until one party could not follow and gave in; it was usually the householder and the Mari Lwyd gained entry to refreshments.

One of the longest-lasting customs was the 'Calenig'. A remnant hardly changed from the time of the Roman occupation along the Welsh borders and the Usk Valley, this consisted of an apple stuck with spices, set on three twig legs and with evergreen sprigs and a candle sometimes. Its name is a Welsh corruption of 'Kalends gift', or New Year gift. Children would take these symbols of good luck around the houses, singing their songs and giving a 'Calenig' in return for small cakes or other gifts.

In some parts of Wales, they celebrated Christmas on 6 January, or 'Old Christmas' as they called it. They disapproved of the Gregorian Calendar of 1752, so reasoned that if they had not lost the days imposed by the new calendar, 6 January would have been the day of Christmas. This custom prevailed particularly in Montgomery, where the Christmas cake was a mild fruit cake piled high with home-candied orange peel; and the Christmas dinner was usually chicken and ham. A sugar pig was a rare treat in the children's stockings for those who were very good.

The people were mostly rural; even those living in the small valley towns had a rural attitude, and many spoke Welsh as their first language. They 'made do'. Their accounts of Christmas are full of warmth and humour. Here is such an account of Christmas in the Swansea valley in the 1920s.

Our chapel stood on top of the bleak Gwrhyd Mountain, in the Swansea Valley. It was the place of worship for the farming families of the district. I used to live on the farm adjoining the chapel and its cemetery.

Our young lives in the 1920s revolved around the chapel and the school at Rhiwfawr. Christmas was very special, as that was the time when our concert was held. Our minister used to come up on two evenings a week along the road from his home two miles away. We would trudge through the mud, sleet and sometimes snow to get to the chapel. There was no electricity, so we used oil lamps; a big coal stove provided warmth.

I remember one Christmas in particular, when it was decided to add more yuletide flavour to our Nativity play and carols by erecting a Christmas tree in the Chapel. It was a beauty, a holly tree with masses of bright red berries. There were no fir trees in our district then – things have changed now as many a reclaimed tip is planted with them.

Presents for hanging on the tree were the next thing. (A prickly business indeed!)

No problem! One of our very dedicated deacons took off on his motorbike and sidecar, for Neath, where he said he could buy gifts usually costing sixpence each [2 new pence] for only fourpence each.

Before hanging them on the tree, numbers were put on each one – even for the girls, odd for the boys – on arrival on THE night, the children were duly given their numbered ticket at the door.

On that occasion, Father Christmas was expected in person. Great excitement. Would he arrive on time, braving the cold? Yes, the minister had received a message – he was on his way. A big knock on the door . . . silence . . . then, in came the old man, bent under his sack of oranges, a great treat at that time. Tumultuous applause for him as he made his way to the big stove to warm his hands, having greeted us all. *Nos waith dda* ('Good evening'), he said, then began to distribute all the presents. Alas, mixed numbers – a

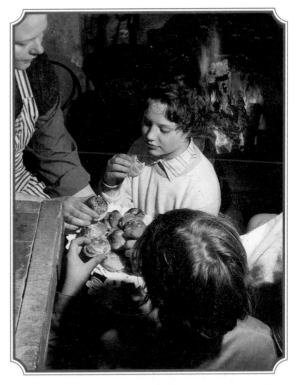

*Enjoying mince pies straight from the seventeenth-century ovens at Penhow Castle,
c. 1980. With thanks to Steven Weekes.*

hefy 12-year-old was seen blushing over his doll and a dainty 5-year-old was in floods of tears when she opened her parcel – a lorry!

More was to come, almost the last boy to receive his gift burst into tears with fright. Forgetting his role, Father Christmas embraced the small boy, saying, '*Paid a llefain Cariad, Dadu sy yara*' ('Don't cry, love, its Dada!').

'Dir nae Christmas noo'

SHETLAND CELEBRATIONS

Margaret Tait

This account was written by Mrs Tait in 1981. It provides an unusual insight into the Christmas activities in the most northerly islands of Great Britain, the Shetlands. Most people associate Scottish custom with New Year, not Christmas – this will set the record straight!
Mr Nicholson, who is the editor of the Shetland Life *magazine, where this piece first appeared, translates the title in Shetland dialect as 'There's no Christmas now'. This is something the old people say at Christmas as a way of suggesting that we do not celebrate the way we used to.*

How often now-a-days, as the Christmas season approaches, and I am in a company of my contemporaries who were children in the mid-1920s, discussion ends with the words, 'Dir nae Christmas noo – every day is a Christmas'.

I suppose it is a sign of approaching old age that I should recently have cast my thoughts backwards through the many years, to the very different circumstances, and indeed the very different town, in which we celebrated Christmas, and have tried to recall the feelings of a little girl, comparatively new to the town, during what is now known as 'The Festive Season'.

Winter, deep winter, was through all my childhood days my favourite time of the year. As a member of a close-knit family living in Lerwick's very first, and at that time only, council 'estate', I loved to come home from school in 'da humin' to find a cheery fire lit in the Modern Mistress range in the living room, and all the 'smucks' warming on the home-made fender box in front of it. Often on opening the door there would be the fragrance of brand-iron bannocks newly made, and of course one could not wait till teatime to enjoy one of these with 'Delova' margarine. (Again this brings memories of walks over the Hillhead to the Danish Dairy Company's shop, and a game of 'pickie' over the counter with Bobby Gray.)

I realise now that there were facets of my own nature which had a lot to do with my preference for the Shetland winter – my liking for reading, for instance. I could very easily, even in the midst of the hubbub of our always crowded room (for our friends were always welcomed) find a corner somewhere and retreat into the fantasy world created by Louisa M. Alcott or Susan Coolidge. However, as often as not I would join in whichever boisterous game was in progress. If we got too noisy my father might look up from his book or newspaper and voice a gentle remonstrance – the only punishment I ever knew him to inflict.

But I digress. Of course, Christmas meant school holidays, always a source of rejoicing. In spite of the efforts of a great many excellent teachers, I never really liked school. Looking back, I realise that this was for the simple reason that I disliked leaving home. In fact I all too easily got off with 'skule-feerie' and must have been the despair of teachers when it came to making up the attendance reports.

There was always plenty to do and I never remember being bored. As a member of a church-going family I would be expected to go to 'practisings' for the children's service to be held in the church, and also for the programme at the annual Sunday-school treat – one of the highlights of the year. For this occasion our devoted teachers and other ladies of the congregation transformed the church hall into a place of light and magic with paper streamers, balloons and crackers. Long tables were set with plates and mugs, and each child was handed a paper bag with our sandwiches and a German bun, which, sadly, I never enjoyed because excitement made me unable to eat. Our Sunday-school superintendent, the late ex-provost P.S. Goodlad, never failed to come and talk to us all. At that time there were no Christmas trees and no gifts were distributed except, perhaps, an apple or orange to take home at the end of the party. But we all went home in a state of happy exhaustion after our games of 'Here's the rovers passing by', 'I sent a letter to my love', 'Out and in the windows' and one which ended each verse with 'Roostie toostie tee-I-Oh!' The parents, who had come after tea to see and hear us perform our practised 'pieces', would be 'daved' for days afterwards with an account of the fun we had had at the party.

One of my joys at the holiday time was to sit in the window and watch for the lamplighter to come along, as another much more distinguished writer had done before me. At that time Lerwick was still gas-lit, with the rather infrequent but much more beautiful street lamps, green-painted, at the kerb edges. The town boundary was then the Burgh Road, but even so it must have been quite a task for one man, on foot and carrying a light ladder, to light up the whole town, and he must have started at early dusk. How quickly and nimbly he scaled the ladder and applied the taper to the incandescent mantles in their glass case, then down to the ground again and on to the next lamp.

Carol-singing in the streets by the Salvation Army is one of my memories – the strains of 'Hark, the herald angels' or 'O come, all ye faithful' would bring us all to the window to watch the small group, one of whom would be playing a concertina, braving the wintry weather to bring us, perhaps, the first taste of the real Christmas and what it was all about.

The afternoon of Christmas Eve was, of course, marked by the appearance of numerous 'peerie guizers'. Much ingenuity had been used in their 'rigging' – the chief considerations were warmth and agility, because it was necessary to call on as many houses as possible in order to fill the 'sock' with donations in both cash and kind. Some children went 'just for fun', but many more were dependent on their 'earnings' of the afternoon for any small treat they might have. Accordingly, they were welcomed at almost every door, and seldom sent away empty, while their 'Happy Christmas!' squeaked through lace-curtain 'masks' seemed to apply equally to giver and receiver. The weather seldom deterred them, and many would still be going around, especially on 'da Street', long after nightfall. In those days, of course, the shops were open till at least six o'clock every evening, and on Saturdays till about eight, Christmas Eve being counted like a Saturday.

Even the shops and tradesmen would enter into the spirit of Christmas giving. The grocer would present every customer with a calendar and a cake. The calendar would be of the pictorial sort, with the name of the firm prominent on it, and would be hung on the kitchen wall in the New Year.

The climax, of course, came late on Christmas Eve with the ceremony of getting out the Santie Claus socks – specially big, seaboot socks which were kept carefully from year to year for this special purpose. It was necessary to make sure that no marauding moth had had a meal off them during their long rest, as Santie would never put anything into a sock that wasn't whole – so many a last-minute stitch was put in just in case. Strangely enough, I remember few details about their contents when the 'Blessed morn' at last arrived – a few sweets, simple games, the longed-for book – at any rate I was never disappointed. This, I realised later, was because so many kind friends and relations had helped Santie along his way.

No long time was spent playing with the new games and toys, however, because breakfast had to be partaken of before we went as a family to the Christmas carols at St Ringan's Church. All my youth the carol service was the highlight of the Christmas season. Not only had a choir, drawn from all the different denominations in town, been practising for weeks to give us this concert, but there would be the small orchestra which Lerwick even then could boast, led by the late Miss Eva Alger, playing before and after the service and during the offertory. At least one small girl in the audience listened and watched enchanted. The minister of St Ringan's in those days was Dr Willcox, and at some point in the recital he would read a 'suitable' extract from a book, perhaps Dickens's *Christmas Carol* – not, as far as I recollect, a Bible reading. On coming out of the usually crowded church, our family would be greeted by others and Christmas wishes were the order of the day. On some occasions, later on, I was to have the privilege of taking part in the St Ringan's Christmas service – an ambition realised.

I remember some fine, frosty weather at Christmas, but only once do I remember a fall of snow during the holidays. This made it a time to be recalled above all others for enjoyment out of doors. Sledging, practically in every street because vehicular traffic was almost non-existent, was indulged in by the small fry on any near-by brae, and by the older and more ambitious on such great runs as Gullets Brae, the Town Hall Brae, Wireless Brae and Braewick Road. Most sledges were home made, though the occasional professionally made toboggan made its appearance too. The fact that there were very few serious accidents must be a tribute to the skill of most of the 'steerers' who sat on the backs of sledges and steered by pressure on long poles. Occasionally a small boy would be seen 'goin' bellygutzer' in the middle of it all. After the passage of so many steel runners, the brae would shine as if polished and the going got faster and faster. The long haul back again up the brae seemed as nothing, in anticipation of the exhilarating flight again to come.

I seem to remember that on both Christmas and New Year's Eves there were a large number of adult guizers around. They would gather at 'da Cross' and circulate among the crowd there until about midnight, when they would disperse to call at the houses of their friends. The sound of the guizer 'bands' in high spirits going from house to house could be heard till morning. This custom seems to have died out, being largely replaced by the Scottish idea of 'first-footing'. Guizing is now mainly kept for the various Up-Helly-A' celebrations throughout the Islands.

A tea-party at my grandparents' house was usually the last notable event in my particular Christmas calendar. More often than not this was on New Year's night, and usually the weather was very bad, so that negotiating the many steps down to the house in one of Lerwick's lanes took time and care. The atmosphere of the old house, the Goss china with coats of arms of many towns, and, later, 'ben', hearing for the first time the faint, imperfect, crackling sound of the 'wireless' – for my uncle was one of the first people in Shetland to own a crystal set – are among my happiest memories.

Christmas every day? Na! Dir nae Christmas noo.

Under the Palms in Ceylon

Miss A. Harp

A teacher in the early years of the twentieth century, Miss Harp recorded the elements of Christmas as experienced by the Ceylonese, Singhalese and Tamil people.

We are all broiling hot at Christmas, and look out our coolest whites to go to church in. A great many of the churches are decorated with Maidenhair ferns and lovely Madonna Lilies. The old Carols and Christmas hymns are translated into Tamil and Singhalese, and even those who do not attend church any other time make a great point of being there at Christmas!

In some of the distant villages, where they cannot get to churches, carol singing is something they take up with great zest; this is carried on in a rather curious way. Pictures of the shepherds, wise men, Christ in the manger and angels praising God are pasted on to a box. The children march through the village singing and carrying the 'Carol box'. It attracts a good deal of attention and the crowd gathers round to hear the stories associated with the pictures.

Buddha's birthday is in May, and the Buddhists have copied the Christian custom of singing carols about the Birth of Christ. At Buddha's birthday, there is great activity among them, and they too parade the streets singing carols to the honour and praise of Buddha.

At Christmas and New Year, there are always cheap fares on the Government railways for the holidays.

In the southern Province of Ceylon it is quite impossible to get a fir tree for a Christmas tree, so an overgrown tea tree or clove tree is generally used. It is decorated with pretty little coloured candles, and toys and gifts.

On New Year's Day the Tamil Christians bring gifts of limes to the missionaries and sing native lyrics to them, introducing the names of the missionaries into the verses of the songs they are singing. Christmas is not usually a day of rest, but certainly a very happy time for everyone.

A South African Picnic

In South Africa picnic parties will spend Christmas Day out in the open, and a famous actress well remembers how she once sat in blazing sunshine on a cliff at the Cape of Good Hope . . . it was Christmas Day. She gazed down upon an amethyst sea and golden sands and dined off cold chicken, strawberries and cream, and the usual summer dishes.

Christmas in India

Marie Kathleen Lenihan

Marie Lenihan is Indian. She might not look it, but she was born to one of those families for whom after several generations of the British Raj India was home. She had no knowledge of 'England's green and pleasant land', and had never seen frost nor snow. Coming to a country that was foreign to her after the partition of 1947 was a great shock. The UK was not home as far as she and thousands like her were concerned.

The elements of her Christmas celebration as a child in the 1920s would seem vaguely familiar to most Westerners, but the social hierarchy and local availability of food and decorations forced an adaptation that seem a lifetime and a continent away from today's experience. Although there are few Indians of European stock left in that vast timeless country of so many customs, her experience is typical for many Christians living in India, regardless of race.

India is a place of distances. Simple tasks like going to mass would become expeditions that required planning. A small household such as ours would still require servants, and they in turn had their own pecking order.

We would spend our Christmases in the hill station of Poona at my grandmother's house. It was always cooler than on the plains, and the countryside was greener. From the time that my cousins joined us, we knew that Christmas was approaching and that soon the great day would be at hand.

The cook who was also Catholic came from Goa. He would never do anything so demeaning as carrying back provisions from the market. He would go off with a boy whose job it was to be the cook's personal pack animal bearing back everything that was needed for the festival. He would appear after making his purchases with the boy carrying a large basket of provisions. Most of the cooking was done in a locally fashioned stove which we called a 'Salamander'.

Fruit bought in the market would be dried in the sunshine. Figs with the bloom still on them, apples, mangoes, oranges, all sorts spread out on steel

A colonial family enjoy Christmas in India, c. 1880s.

trays covered with wire gauze to keep the birds off. Even so, we children would play outside keeping an eye out for the kites who would fly down and steal any item of food. I particularly loved the figs which I would hold by their stalks and squeeze into my mouth. We would make our own candied peel, and if we were doing anything to assist with the making of the Christmas pudding, my grandmother would insist that we whistled a tune, because she knew that we could not take sly nibbles while we were whistling!

We would always try to have a turn at stirring the big milk bowls of mixture which gave us the opportunity of 'scraping off' the generously left mixture, but always with the warning not to eat much in case we got stomach ache.

We did not have turkey, although once we had a peacock. Most often it was guinea fowl who would scratch around the garden, never noticing when their numbers became depleted as Christmas approached. We had a great big fireplace outside made from large bricks that must have measured 36 in x 36 in x 24 in high. The Christmas pudding would be placed on this to boil for 8–10 hours, in a large black iron pot.

Decorations and greenery would be brought in from various sources. The doctors at the local hospital always managed to get mistletoe (so they would have an excuse to kiss any pretty girl!). We always were given some, and this would be put up together with the other decorations. A large tamarind tree (also known as 'Flame of the Forest') which dominated our compound would be decorated as well with paper Chinese lanterns hanging on its lower branches. These would be lit on Christmas Eve. Having hung up our stockings we would need no urging to go to bed because we believed that Christmas Day would come sooner if we did.

We used to hear the grown-ups being driven off to St Patrick's Cathedral which saw four generations of our family marry there, and 'live happily ever after'. Miriam our Indian Ayah stayed until after the grown-ups returned from midnight mass in the carriage with the stars overall and accompanied by many old friends for the first toast of Christmas Day. They would also have the first slice of Christmas cake. We almost always stirred at this point and would be allowed to have a slice of cake and a lemonade each. The climax was being able to open our Christmas stockings!

At Tiffin (or mid-day meal) as a special treat, a second table was added to the large one so we could sit with the grown-ups. The Christmas pudding was brought in to us all aglow with flaming brandy. This was great fun for us as we were permitted to play a version of 'snapdragons' by attempting to steal a piece of fruit from the pudding while it was alight. We all looked for 2 or 8 Anna pieces which were hidden like sixpences and shillings in the Christmas pudding. Finding one meant good luck.

Later in the day we went with our ayah to the Gymkhana Club to meet Father Christmas, who arrived at dusk, heralded with beating drums and clashing cymbals, bearing two huge sacks brimming with toys, riding on a camel. Our names would be called, and we were given our respective gifts.

After that we were driven back through the shopping centre where in one shop stood a huge Father Christmas in a snow scene handing gifts to children. I shall never forget this memory!

Later we went to mass and our cathedral had the Nativity scene with life-sized figures, but the crib had no snow. It was decorated with green palms and the scarlet poinsettia flowers, which were THE Christmas flower.

Many years later in that same cathedral Father Alborghetti preached a Christmas sermon in which he stated that Christ was an Oriental and not an Occidental figure. For although he came and was meant for all of us, his children, he was born in Bethlehem which was in the Orient. I thought how appropriate all the green palms and poinsettia flowers were!

At that time in the East the stars were always so brilliant at Christmas. I believed that we could see the Christmas Star shining huge as it twinkled. It was the essence of a happy childhood memory!

Australian Sunshine

Christmas in a hot climate does not involve sitting around a fire and telling stories – the Australians are more likely to be having a picnic on the beach for Christmas. The whole emphasis of Christmas has been shifted to the outdoors in fact, with Christmas cards showing white beaches, blue cloudless skies and waters, sunny plains and spreading gum trees, although there is a current trend towards celebrating the Western 'White Christmas' with Santa Claus, holly and 'snow'. In Melbourne there is a huge Santa Claus procession every year. Poor Santa must be melting under all that velvet and fur in the heat of the Australian summer!

Christmas gifts in Australia are usually exchanged at breakfast, and many still attend church afterwards. There are two plants particularly associated with Australian Christmas, the Christmas Bush and the Christmas Bell. These are bought to adorn homes together with ferns and palm leaves. The Bell is a huge golden bell-shaped flower with bright glossy green leaves. In the 1960s some families began to adorn these plants with tinsel. They also have a tinsel-strewn Christmas Tree – and put tinsel along the backs of furniture, including the chairs, which may have made them difficult to sit on. One Australian innovation at Christmas time is carols in the park. Thousands of people gather in city parks to sing carols by the light of torch flares and candles.

Early pioneers in Australia experienced quite a different sort of Christmas. The following diary entry recorded by the botanist on Captain James Cook's ship, *Endeavour*, which went in search of 'The unknown lands of the Australis' in 1769, is the first account of an (almost) Australian Christmas:

24th – Land in sight . . . Calm most of the day. Myself in a boat shooting, in which I had good success, killing, chiefly several Gannets or Solan Geese so like European ones that they are hardly distinguishable from them. As it was the humour of the ship to keep Christmas in the old fashioned way it was resolved of them to make a Goose pye for the morrow.

25th Our Goose pye was eat with great approbation and in the Evening all hands were as Drunk as our forefathers used to be upon the like occasion.

An account of Christmas recorded in a newspaper of 1884 reported the following:

It may assist our readers in England to form some idea of what Christmas is in Australia, by reminding them of what it is not!

The festival does not occur at a period of the year when days are at their shortest, and the weather is at its coldest; when nature is bound in ice, or muffled in snow; when noses are blue, and coughs and colds plentiful: when the sun shines with dull red light for an hour and a half in the middle of the day. . . . No, with us nature holds high festival at Christmas-tide as well as man. Our orchards are ruddy with fruit, our gardens bright with flowers, and our fields golden with the yellowing harvest, at the very time we observe the greatest holiday of the year. It comes to us in the full flush of midsummer, and it is celebrated in the open air. It is prolonged merrymaking, for there is suspension of all business from Christmas Eve until the morrow of New Year's Day. The old year passes away, and its successor is ushered in with general rejoicing. We have not lost the capacity for hard work, but as the earnings of all classes are sufficient to provide for something more than the satisfaction of our daily wants, we can afford to make holiday at Christmas, and to do so in a genial, generous and ungrudging spirit. . . . There is a thoroughly festive

character about all such celebrations here. No anxious considerations impair the artisan's enjoyment
in Australia. He is prosperous, and
all his prospects are encouraging.

A Christmas dinner in Australia
necessarily takes the shape of an al
fresco meal. It is eaten under green
boughs, like the 'feast of tabernacles'
among the ancient Israelites. Our artist
has selected for one of his subjects of
illustration a party of merrymakers
setting out from a Christmas picnic;
and as the neighbourhood of
Melbourne abounds with public parks,
and in pleasantly situated reserves,
available for purposes of recreation,
pleasure seekers enjoy a wide range of
choice as to locality.

A contemporary Australian picnic, from the
Illustrated Melbourne Post, *1866.*

One of the most popular places of
resort is the beach at Brighton which is
only half an hour's ride by railway from Melbourne, and is visited by
thousands of people on Christmas Day. An impromptu encampment
springs up among the teatree scrub which flourishes upon the sand
hummocks. Fires are lit, hampers of provisions unpacked, tablecloths are
spread upon the sand, awnings rigged overhead (against the heat of the
sun), and innumerable parties apply themselves to diminish the stocks of
comestibles and drinkables they have brought with them. The clatter of
plates, popping of corks, jingling of glasses and the rattle of knives and
forks mingle with the merry peals of laughter, with the buzz of
conversation, and the splash of the waves upon the beach. As there is little
formality in the social intercourse of colonists, so there is little reticence or
restraint. . . .

They betake themselves after dinner to games of cricket, quoits, kiss
in the ring, dancing and other pastimes. . . . As a matter of course where
holidaymakers congregate, thither also resort itinerant fruit-sellers,

musicians, confectioners, vendors of gingerbeer and lemonade, water-carriers, and the professors of all sorts of minor industries, so that the outskirts of the encampment somewhat resembles an English Village Fair. . . .

Everybody is well dressed, and nothing strikes a stranger so much as the evidences of well-being which are furnished by the personal attire of all classes of Christmas holidaymakers. And, falling as the festival does, at midsummer, the lightest and brightest garments are donned for the occasion.

New Zealand's Sun, Surf and the Pohutakawa Tree

Christmas comes to New Zealand in the middle of hot summer. Like the Australians, the New Zealanders spend their Christmas holidays on the beach. The shops are decorated with all the traditional elements of Western Christmas, snow and glitter, tinselly snowscenes – and poor old Father Christmas swelters in the heat as he presides over his grotto. This is because the parents and grandparents of today's young New Zealanders came from European communities, and their traditions are a nostalgic reminder of home.

The blossoms of the Pohutakawa tree, which is the New Zealand Christmas tree, adorn every home. Nowadays most families will also have a pine tree, decorated with candles. The Christmas pudding is served with ice-cream and fruit salad containing summer fruits such as strawberries.

From Christmas Day through to New Year, New Zealanders get into their cars, or put on their backpacks, and go travelling. They usually take their summer vacation during the Christmas period when schools have the long summer break, so it is the perfect opportunity to travel.

Surf bathers enjoy the Christmas holidays at the Mount, Tauranga, East North Island, New Zealand, 1933. Auckland Weekly News.

As in Britain, there are parties arranged for under-privileged children and adults. The children's events are held outdoors with fancy dress parades and races just like a summer carnival – except that there are groups of carol singers and Salvation Army bands alongside the ice-cream vans and salad buffets.

In the home, the traditional Christmas fare prevails. Most have a bird of some kind on the Christmas Day table, with the traditional vegetables and mince pies. These will be flanked by cold cuts, salads and cold desserts and fruit.

Children put up their stocking for Father Christmas to fill on Christmas Eve. Parents go to the midnight services, and all attend the many carol services both in the churches and outdoors. But there is no snow, no cherry noses muffled in scarves and furry hoods, no short days and long dark evenings to inspire storytelling and games, for this is Christmas in summertime – Christmas in New Zealand.

A Hungarian Musical Christmas

AND CHRISTMAS IN BULGARIA BY IVAILO PANGAROV

Helena de Pettes

My mother had six children. I was five years old, the youngest. On the afternoon of Christmas Eve we dressed as prettily as possible . . . a white world! Outside the snow was lying deep. Our horse-drawn sledge was waiting to take us with our nanny to the theatre for the festive pantomime. On arriving back home we found the house glittering with decorations; the dining room table was prepared for a delicious tea, including the traditional poppyseed and nut rolls, chocolate cream log, and other delicacies. My parents usually invited a few cousins and some orphans to share our warm hospitality. We had hardly finished our meal when we heard the ringing of chimes and bells. Then, our mother announced that angels were arriving, bringing gifts and a Christmas tree from heaven, celebrating the day when Jesus Christ our Saviour was born.

Our family proceeded towards the drawing room, which was like fairy-land. In the middle of the room stood the glittering Christmas tree, as tall as the high-ceilinged room, with a brilliant star on top. . . . All around were angels in white dresses singing, 'Dics seg' – 'Hosanna in the Highest!'

We all knelt down. My father played the violin, my mother the piano; they

The de Pettes family enjoy a traditionally musical Hungarian Christmas Eve, 1934. Courtesy of Helena de Pettes.

played 'Mennybl az Angyal', a Hungarian Christmas carol telling us of the angels heralding the birth of the King of Kings.

While our admiration was focused on the crib we were dumb-struck with deep emotion and, as the angels disappeared leaving an array of gifts, I was, perhaps, carried up to bed.

Christmas in Bulgaria – Ivailo Pangarov

In Bulgaria we have customs which are part of our culture. On the table on Christmas Eve there have to be seven, nine or thirteen different kinds of food. There is symbolic meaning in these numbers. For example, the number thirteen is because of the number of Jesus and his Apostles. We also have the custom that men dressed in fur coats and with Christmas 'sticks' in their hands go round the houses, and they are welcomed by the hosts. In the house they sing Christmas songs and bless the hosts. In return the 'Christmas men' receive money or gifts. Sometimes they get doughnuts, which they put on their sticks. Another custom is when the family get together around the Christmas table they have to sit on the floor. That is because during the Secret Dinner Jesus and the apostles also sat on the floor.

At the South Pole

During Christmas two small groups of people residing in the Polish polar stations, far away from their homes, observe the most important holiday in their solitude. The only companions they have are the animals, who during Bethlehem night speak in human voices. At both polar stations the Christmas Eve feast starts at 5 p.m. local time. Everything seems similar to a regular Christmas observance. The only difference is the scenery outside. At Spitzbergen there is a midwinter and ever-deep polar night during the whole day. At Antarctica in the middle of summer, the whole day is sunny. At midnight on 24 and 25 December, the improvised *Pasterka* takes place. The small chapel is in snow decor, attached to ice-rocks disguised as a temple.

This version of Christmas seems different. The loneliness can be sensed in spite of the presence of dozens of friends from the station. The absence of the real home, the closest people and the real joy which accompanies those holidays . . .

Though the distance is long, all station residents can spend some time with their beloved ones. Both stations have radio or satellite communications allowing everybody a few minutes' conversation with their closest at home. The fast exchange of sentences, everybody wants to say as much as possible, each wants to talk. Exchange of wishes, short conversation about the dinner menu, weather, we have plenty of snow – you have again a warm dark winter . . . have to finish, the next colleague is waiting and the next . . .

Everyone feels for at least a short time the warmth of their home emitted. Afterwards they gather together and share their impressions from the conversations they have had.

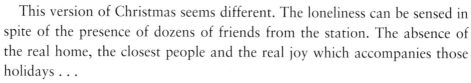

RELIGIOUS CEREMONIES

The Oldest Celebration of All – in Ethiopia

Christianity reached Abyssinia (or Ethiopia) in AD 330 or perhaps even earlier. The Christians there are Copts and their rituals date right back to the earliest days of the Christian Church.

The Coptic diocese holds a first-century icon, which is revered and believed to be a true likeness of the Virgin Mary painted by St Luke. It is only brought out once every hundred years because of its fragility. In the twelfth century a copy was made which is displayed in the great church of the Archbishop Gregorius in Egypt from whom most of the following information came. The observance of Christmas in his Church is far more restrained, and more in line with the celebrations and rituals of the Orthodox Christians, but the following describes how the most ancient Church of all celebrates.

The observances of the seasons centre around the Church, and the traditions which are observed all relate to the seasonal celebration, whether of a practical nature or a religious – there seems to be little distinction between the two. The oldest churches are hewn from the very rocks, built in a square shape with an outside court. Though the churches may be simple and the altars made from wood, they will always have a few pieces of finer material in them, marble, even gold. The Tabernacle, or Ark, is of gold studded with precious stones.

The Holy place of Ethiopia, the Jerusalem, is at a place called Lalibela. To this place, at Christmas time, come pilgrims from every corner of Ethiopia, some travelling on foot for days or weeks to get there. There on the hilltops they stay, camping where they sit, chanting and praying away the vigil hours until the dawn of Christmas Day, when there is a procession from another church on another hilltop. The colourful procession makes its way, sun glittering on the costly robes of the clergy as they head the procession behind the whipmen. These are young men with whips, which they lash from side to side to keep the procession in line, and to keep the pilgrims from breaking through the lines. The procession is a magnificent sight with literally thousands of monks, nuns and laity following behind the clergy.

Reaching their destination on the Lalibela hillside, a service is held in the rites of the Coptic Catholic Church. After which, the priests bless bread and water, wine or other drink, and a meal is given to the multitudes, in remembrance of the feeding of the multitude on the Mount.

Religious observances over, the pilgrims begin the 'Birthday' celebrations. Sports are a major part, and the young men particularly have races and strength feats of all kinds. Feasting and dancing and singing are enjoyed by all.

In the Carpathian Mountains

Maria   Hubert   and   others

This account of a Byzantine Christian Christmas in the mountains of Eastern Slovakia comes from the Byzantine Catholic Church of St Philip the Apostle. The Byzantine rite is half way between Roman and Orthodox Catholicism and their practices are among the most ancient and original Christian practices in the world. All the traditions we observe today began with a religious observance, which became a habit – a custom. In the Byzantine Church many of these observances are still apparent in their Christmas traditions. The Christmas Eve meal begins with the mother sprinkling everyone with Holy Water and the father then takes the Holy Water to the animals, domestic and farm. Twelve dishes are laid on the table to represent the twelve apostles, and an empty place is set for an unexpected but welcomed guest, perhaps a member of the family who cannot be present – or even Christ Himself, in response to the 'No Room at the Inn' story.

To understand Christmas in the Carpathian region of Eastern Europe, it would be necessary to know that all the festivities begin after the Church services for 25 December/7 January. All that precedes is done in quiet preparation. There are no carols, no parties nor many of the external trappings of Western society and culture.

Since every village and country has its own variations of how to celebrate Christmas, it would be difficult to describe every custom and tradition in detail; for this reason we speak here about the customs prevalent in what is now the Zemplyn district of Eastern Slovakia.

With the 'St Philip's Fast' beginning 15/28 November, prayer and fasting become the way of life – set aside for only the most necessary reasons. One of the breaks in this is the Feast of St Nicholas. It is on this day that gifts are given.

Certainly not the extravagant types of gifts children find so appealing, but fruits, nuts, simple toys, books or other worthwhile items. The concept of the gift was to convey the idea that we receive what we need, not always or only what we want or desire. The generous soul responsible for the gift-giving, known to us as St Nicholas, has been translated into Santa Claus. The real St Nicholas was a fourth-century Bishop of Asia Minor (now part of Turkey), known for his generosity and financial aid to those who were in desperate situations. He has become the patron saint of children, several occupations – sailors, pawnbrokers among them – and the entire Byzantine Church. The familiar three-ball insignia of the pawnbroker has come down from a legend that the saintly Bishop saved three daughters of a townsman from prostitution by mysteriously supplying a bag of gold – tossed through an open window at night – for the dowry of each, which they found at the foot of their beds when they awoke.

An East European peasant icon of the Nativity, c. 1800.

After the brief levity of St Nicholas, the tenor of the prayer and fasting resumes. There are no carols sung yet – they await the announcement of Christ's birth at the church services of Christmas Eve. At home, at the sight of the first star in the heavens that evening, a special Holy Supper – of meatless dishes – is had. Then the tree is decorated with candles, fruits and nuts (if there is a tree to decorate at all).

All the anticipation of the forty days' fasting comes to a conclusion with the Divine Liturgy of Christmas Day itself, when the festive meats and other foods are eaten after the services have been attended.

Now come the carols. Now comes the festive celebration. Now come the joyous festivities – visiting friends with the salutation 'Christ is Born!' to be answered by 'Glorify Him!'

This time of rejoicing lasts for two weeks and is capped with the observance of the Feast of Theophane, celebrating the Baptism of Christ in the River Jordan by John the Baptist – at which event Christ's Divinity was revealed.

In Search of the Place of the Nativity – Bethlehem

Edited from several sources

Requests for comments on the theme 'Christmas in Bethlehem' brought in such a wealth of information that it would take a book to relate! A selection of the best, to include a background picture together with customs observed and events remembered, has been compiled from the accounts of Dr Eli Rosen, Fr Marcello OFM, Sister Frances Teresa, Joan Greathead and Marie Alexander and translated and edited by myself.

Bethlehem, a small town nestling in the valley, with a skyline of church spires, dome-topped mosques and spiky minarets.

At Christmastide, pilgrims from all over the Christian world descend on the little town, to celebrate the two-thousand-year-old mystery in the Church of the Nativity. Long before Ecumenism, this holy place brought Christians of all denominations together to worship, for it is in the grotto beneath this ancient church that Jesus is believed to have been born.

Not an idle or legendary belief either, because the place has been marked and documented for all of that two thousand years. As early as AD 135, the Emperor Hadrian, who was made emperor after his successful generalship – Hadrian's Wall his lasting achievement in Britain – erected a temple to Adonis over the site of the cave, in an attempt to stop people worshipping the Christian God there. However, he did the Christians a good turn rather than a bad one, because he marked for centuries the site, which otherwise might have been lost in the many battles, building and general domestic life of Bethlehem.

In the early fourth century Empress Helena, a Christian Roman who devoted her whole life to searching for the holy places and relics of the time of Christ's ministry on earth, ordered the demolition of Hadrian's temple and the excavation of the original grotto of the Nativity. It was her son,

Constantine the Great, who erected the first Basilica of the Nativity over the site. Hardly anything of this building remains today, as most of it was rebuilt in the sixth century, and most of the present building dates from that time.

Since the time of the Crusades, the Franciscans have had charge of looking after the Basilica. St Francis of Assisi had made a friend out of Saladin, because Saladin felt that Francis was a man who lived by the teachings of his God, while all around were soldiers shedding the blood of his people in the name of a God of peace! A phenomenon which must have been difficult for this great Muslim philosopher to understand. So, the followers of Francis were allowed to keep their peace within the city walls looking after the place of the Nativity and its Basilica, and as peace took over from the fighting, they stayed. Today there are Greek and Armenian Orthodox communities who share the responsibility and maintain different parts of the great building for their own groups to use.

But the place of the actual cave is still cared for by Franciscans. It is a small area by comparison with the huge edifice built around it over the centuries, measuring only about 12 by 40 ft. It is reached by a narrow stairway, and its walls are hung with rich but ancient tapestries smelling of incense and age, the overriding first impression being the dozens of silver and gilt votive lamps hanging all over the ceiling. In an alcove, over which there is an altar, is placed in the floor a huge silver fourteen-point star bearing the simple inscription, *Hic, de Virgine Maria Jesus Christus natus est* – 'Here, of the Virgin Mary, Jesus Christ was born'.

Peaceful, cool and dark, it is a perfect place for quiet reflection, with just the sound of the feet of the multitude of pilgrims who come from every corner of the world. . . . Until midnight, that is. Then the church fills to bursting point ready for the midnight services. The three main groups take it in turns, the Orthodox services taking place after the Catholic one, which is the one which all Western Christians attend, whatever their denomination. Then, the acoustics of the massive structure carry the songs and the chants on waves and echoes into every corner and beyond the great doors into the square, carrying one along on a great upsurge of joy and the feeling of continuity with millions of pilgrims of 2,000 years, standing on the same ground with the same purpose.

Unfortunately, the town in the daytime can be a bit of a shock to many pilgrims. On the one hand, time really does seem to stand still. The dress of the people, the habits and customs, even the donkeys bearing their burdens through the narrow streets. There is an air of peace in the place, Jew, Muslim and Christian walking side by side, *muezzin* chants mingling with plainsong. Modestly robed women carry their shopping alongside jeans-clad tourists. You have to look for the Bethlehem beneath the hustle and bustle of souvenir-hunting, camera-snapping tourists. The 5,000 inhabitants of the Bethlehem of Christ's day are swelled to more than a hundred times that figure today, and cars vie with the donkeys for road space.

One of the overriding memories of most visitors is the enormous number of cars and buses, especially the cavalcades of traffic on all roads leading into Bethlehem, made up or dust tracks, which begin early on the morning of the 24th carrying thousands of people into Bethlehem for the services of Christmas Eve. Even the war years did not stop that, with servicemen from both sides coming together to celebrate the great feast of Peace.

Today, modern carol singers sing in Bethlehem streets, but out on the hillside, still, the shepherds tend their flocks, as they have done for over two millennia; and in the silence of the night, the sounds of the town dulled by the wind playing through the grasses, you can imagine you can hear the age-old message of the angels' song,

'Glory to God in the Highest, and on Earth, peace, to ALL men'.

Magyar Christmas

From A Peep at Hungary and other sources

Hungary has some of the most ancient customs dating back thousands of years, which have been adapted to the Christian Christmas festival. Many were almost lost as a result of many decades of Communism, which forbade the making of Christmas cribs, or any other overt or religious form of celebration.

One of these customs is the Christmas Canticles which were sung during Advent and Christmas. Strange and ancient chants which have been handed down as an oral tradition for so many centuries no one seems to know when they began. They imitate the sounds of the rocking of a cradle, or a war march; another tells the story of how all living things were around the manger trying to lull the baby Jesus to sleep with their own sounds. You can hear the crowing of the cock, the neighing of the horse, the braying of an ass, the roaring of a lion and so on.

On 6 January, Feast of the Epiphany, it is the time for the Starboys who went around from home to home with their portable Nativity crib scene covered with a cloth. For a gift of cake, money or fruit, they would take off the cover and show the crib. Sometimes these were organized by the local church, and the cribs were

The Nativity players carrying their Nativity with them around the villages, from a nineteenth-century illustration.

cleverly made by local artisans. The boys would carry a paper star with a candle in it. Others dressed as the Three Kings to follow the star as they went carolling around the town on their way to find the Christchild. They are usually accompanied by a priest, who blesses the houses with incense. On the great gates of the Hungarian Castle of Biskra is a small plaque which reads, 'In 1778 the Magyan Kings passed by and blessed this house'. The Three Kings are greatly venerated in Hungary and many myths and legends have grown up around the cult.

Tekla, in *Domitor*, has the following comments to make of yet another variation of this custom: 'The popular Nativity plays in Hungary are centred around amusing jokes, songs and acts performed by shepherds dressed in huge fur capes worn inside out. The Nativity players carry a home-made manger with them or a small house in the shape of a church. Nowadays it is the children who perform the plays, except for one or two Szekely villages in East Transylvania, where grown-up men present the miracle plays, with the peculiar addition of formidable masks made of animal skins worn by the shepherds. . . . There are two types of Nativity plays, those with actors and those with puppets. The latter is known as the Dancing Puppet Nativity play and has two regional centres in Hungary.'

In the cradle-rocking ceremony an elaborately decorated cradle is placed in front of the church altar and, while the many verses of the carol are sung, the congregation file up to rock the cradle, one by one. This may sound a little silly to the sophisticated minds of today, but to past generations, whose minds had not been so broadened by telecommunications, the internet and the worldwide web, it was intended to bring them closer to the atmosphere of that first Christmas night.

While the custom has disappeared, and the few remaining rocking cribs are in museum collections such as the Bayerische Nationalmuseum in Munich, and the Christmas Archives, the carols remain and come from many countries as well as from Hungary, where the custom is thought to have begun. Czechoslovakia also has a rocking carol, well known as 'We will rock you'. The German version is 'Joseph Dearest, Joseph Mine', while the Polish rocking carol is 'Lulay Jesu'.

Christmas with a Spanish Flavour in the 1960s

Maria Hubert

Many years ago I had the advantage of completing my education in Spain. What impressed me most, as a student with a strong interest in history, was the different festivals.

Being a Catholic country, most of Spain's festivals were based around a religious event. There were street parades with clergy and choirs in full regalia, bands and performers. I remember once walking down a street and suddenly coming across a crowd on the corner. They were watching a colourful parade going by, with religious banners, a magnificent silver gilt cross and about a dozen men sweating under the weight of a great Madonna and Child. It looked like a medieval pageant – it was, in fact; a custom which had not changed for centuries.

Christmas tended to be a fairly low-key religious affair. The build-up was one of fasting and abstinence, extra visits to church, etc. On Christmas Eve there was a midnight mass, and even the poorest church was beautifully filled with flowers, the pinewood polished until it was like burnished gold and candles everywhere. Every child and available male who could hold a musical note in the parish seemed to be called upon to sing in the choir, and carols began about an hour before the mass.

A feature of old Spain, particularly in the south, was the Bellmen. These were groups of strolling players, the troubadours of olden times in fact. The famous flamenco singer, José Meneze, remembers 'the Bellmen of my youth. They would stroll around the towns singing carols and playing their tambourines and guitars. They had a deep influence on my music.' Their music was essentially Spanish, and they told stories of the Holy Family in their *villancicos*, which were carols and songs about the Nativity story.

Many places had a Nativity play in song, which was also called *villancico*. It followed Joseph and Mary to the inn, thence to the stable where the Baby was born to the song of angels. The shepherds come from the fields, the Kings in great splendour, and finally the *Huida*, the Flight into Egypt. This play was often shown before the mass. Occasionally, the mass would stop after the creed and, before the serious consecration began, the play would be performed.

One rather modern Augustinian priest told me it was so that those who would not otherwise come early enough to see the play, had no choice but to watch it if it was in the middle of the mass! He may have had a point. Spain in the early 1960s still had a large population of illiterate people and the only way to get them to understand what they were celebrating was to show them by acting out the Bible stories. This was similar to the English Church in the Middle Ages.

Some rural customs are so ancient one wonders where they came from, and I traced the customs of one area back to the third-century liturgy. In Álava province, the event I remember, began with shepherds who gathered in front of the mayor's house to sing carols. They were led by the oldest shepherd who carried a lamb, and a young shepherdess carrying a dressed wooden model of the Baby Jesus. The mayor and his council and then the parishioners followed the shepherds to the church, all singing, where they were greeted by the priest who blessed them all. Then the shepherds performed a ritualistic dance in front of the church. This was quite stately and involved the beating of the ground with sticks. The singing and dancing then continued all through the service, and afterwards the priests lit a bonfire and a ritual meal was offered to the Christchild, still in the arms of the shepherdess. The custom survives today, but nowadays this is a 'pretend' meal. When I was there, a special vegetable soup was made by the women of the parish in a huge kettle or cauldron. This was symbolically offered first to the Christchild, then to everyone else, which was a way of breaking the long Christmas fast, as many people had not eaten all day.

The Christmas tree was rarely seen. At least, I never saw even one, despite being fortunate enough to visit homes of many 'classes', both urban and rural. But the Christmas crib was always in evidence in every home. Christmas markets began to appear in the market squares, selling all manner of notions to make Christmas cribs. One might sell sheets of wood and cork for making stables, another had small figurines for those who could not make their own. Almost every home was involved in making, setting up or improving their old Nativity sets every year. Rich and poor alike, parents, grandparents and children all join in this central part of the Christmas preparation.

Whereas the crib sellers were the only main stalls in a pre-Christmas market when I was there in the 1960s, and the food and toy stalls appeared after Christmas Day in anticipation for the celebrations on 6 January, now the stalls are selling all manner of things before Christmas. The *turrón* seller was always very popular and still is. *Turrón* is a kind of nougat made from almonds and honey. There is a soft kind too called *turrón jijona*, which is more like marzipan in texture and kinder on the teeth, but is still rich and delicious, and in Mallorca they have their own speciality made from hazelnuts, *turrón de avellana*, which was my particular favourite.

Sometimes, vendors would go from house to house selling *turrón*, and it was considered unlucky not to buy. There are many stories and legends surrounding this most ancient sweetmeat. Some say that it was originally an offering to the goddess Baalat in Asia Minor and was brought to Spain by the Carthaginians a thousand years before Christ was born. Others place the

The arrival of the Magi in Madrid, c. 1930s.

custom with the Romans, who would give the sweet as a New Year Gift, and yet others say it came with the Arab invasion in the eighth century.

It was common to give tradespeople gifts if their work was appreciated. Postmen got money from the townsfolk, and from the farms, such as Son Guells in Mallorca where I stayed; they would get hams, olives, cheeses, etc. It was not an uncommon sight to see the traffic policemen on their little islands, surrounded with gifts of wine, fruits, cheeses and hams.

After Christmas Day itself excitement began to increase as on 6 January the Three Kings visited the markets and left gifts for children at their homes while on their way to visit the Christchild. Now it is getting common for children to ask Santa Claus and then ask the Three Kings if Santa does not bring what they want! But in the 1960s only the Kings brought gifts, and children did not expect anything until after the religious ceremonies were over.

The First Christmas Crib

The following account I have freely translated from the original Latin by the chronicler of the Life of St Francis, Thomas Da Celano, who lived from 1229 to 1257.
It tells the story of how we came to have representations of the Nativity in our homes and churches and public places at Christmastime. The story itself can be more charmingly narrated without the confines of Celano's account. But many believe the story to be an unsubstantiated legend, so by going back to the source of the story it may be proved to be not a legend, but a true account.

With reverential memory we recall that three years before his glorious death what he did on the feast of the birth of our Lord Jesus Christ.

There was living in the land a man named John, of meritorious life, whom Francis loved for his noble and honourable ways and spirit. Fifteen days before Christmas he went to this man and said, 'If you like we can present, for this Feast, in memory of the Child who was born in Bethlehem, a representation of the uncomfortable way he came into the world, laid in a manger with an ass and an ox nearby.'

Francis wanted the people to prepare more diligently for the Coming of Christ at Christmas, by showing them what it must have been like on that first Christmas night in a lowly stable at Bethlehem. He wanted to bring Bethlehem to Grecchio. He created a manger, and brought an ox and a donkey to the place where he was to celebrate the Christmas Mass.

The night was illuminated like day and men and animals came to the new mystery. The air resounded with silver voices, and jubilant responses. The holy brothers sang praises to God; the whole night resulted in jubilation . . . he celebrated the solemn Mass over the manger, and enjoyed once more the consolation of his priesthood.

Francis began to tell the story of the first Nativity. He described the place of the nativity in Bethlehem as he himself had seen it when some years earlier he spent time in the Holy Land, and made friends with the great Saladin, who respected the humble friar as he respected no other 'infidel'. It was said that the sermon which Francis gave to the people of Grecchio on the hillside that night, illuminated by the torches they carried, was so eloquent that many believed they saw the Baby Jesus in the manger.

After the death of St Francis, the friars consecrated an altar on the spot where he had brought the story of the Nativity alive on that special night. Shortly afterwards, it became popular to have a representation of the Holy Family in the churches at Christmastime.

St Francis and the Mass of the Christmas Crib by Patricia Fallace, the Nativitist, 1990.

Later the wealthy began to have figures made for their homes, and the custom spread with the Franciscan friars as they travelled the world with their missionary zeal.

One of the oldest sets of Nativity figures belonged to Queen Elizabeth of Hungary, herself a Franciscan. It is in the convent of the Poor Clare Nuns in Krakow, Poland, where she ended her days in the thirteenth century.

Italians are still among the best and most famous crib-makers in the world, and at Christmastime, the Christmas markets are full of little figures, which people collect to add to their family Nativity set, making it larger each year or generation.

The Pifferari

Translated and told by Florence and Edith Scannell

The following extract is of a typical Victorian story of sadness and hope, but there the similarity ends. Being an Italian story, there is a happy ending, with the young boy turning out to be Crezina's long-lost brother and his foster mother getting well again. In between the melodrama is an excellent account of the customs of the Pifferari, the Italian shepherds who keep up the traditions of serenading the Baby Jesus in commemoration of those first shepherds of Bethlehem, and a typical visit to a church to see the Christmas crib.

'*Eccoli*, there they are, Bettina! I want to go and see them . . .' and off rushed little Crezina, the only child of the Marchese di San Renato.

Bettina hurried after her charge who was watching the road which was several feet below the garden. In the wall was one of those niches containing a small group of the Virgin and Child, so often seen in Italy. Crezina knelt on the marble seat and leant her elbows on the wall, listening eagerly to the sound of the bagpipes, or *zampogni*, as the Italians called them. She knew it was the custom of some of the peasants to come round at Christmas time, and play a strange sweet melody before the images of the Virgin and Child placed in any open place on the road. They say it is the old tune that the shepherds played on their way to Bethlehem after the visit of the Angels, announcing the birth of Jesus Christ.

The air has never been set to music, but is taught by one generation of Pifferari to another, so is not forgotten, and the duty is never left undone. People give the wandering musicians food and money, but they never actually ask for anything. They are there out of a time-honoured tradition, to welcome the Baby Jesus.

Crezina had spent her winters generally in Rome, and had never before heard the Pifferari play their Christmas melody. 'Look, Bettina, here are the Pifferari come to play before our Madonnina! I wonder if they have come from far away; they look tired don't they?'

'I dare say they have walked many miles this morning, *poverini*. One of them is only a lad.'

The two musicians raised their hats and began their music. Crezina listened, absorbed, and fixed her eyes eagerly on the faces of the Pifferari. The elder man had a rugged, bronzed face, with an honest kindly expression, so often met with among the peasants in Italy. But he did not attract her attention so much as his intellectual-looking companion. A boy of twelve or so, with a beautiful dark face, eyes like black velvet and a red flushing of his cheeks as he glanced upwards at the signorina, but which soon died away leaving him tired and weary looking.

One of the Pifferari, traditional Italian shepherds who played their bagpipes at the street creche, c. 1890.

'Bettina, run quickly and ask papa to give me something for the Pifferari,' said Crezina, turning to the maid.

Bettina went off and soon returned with some money, and the musicians were to come into the kitchen for some refreshment.

'Do you know, Bettina, I asked the Pifferari their names, and the old man is Michele, and the boy is Giovanni and he is not his son but a sort of cousin and he has never been a Pifferari before. They come from a village high up in the mountains, quite a long way off.'

'*Daverro, Signorina*, you have quite made acquaintance with the lad! He seems a nice gentle boy, and they are very grateful for the rest and food.'

Crezina was ready to go to church with her father at two o'clock, and ran to take his hand when he called her. It was a lovely day; the sun shone bright and warm, and only when they were on the shady side of the street did they remember that it was midwinter, for there the light wind brought with it a sharpness and chill from the distant snow-covered mountains, and

Crezina felt the comfort of the warm jacket which she had scarcely allowed Bettina to put on her.

The Marchese was a tall slender man with a rather sad expression on his face, which brightened up however when he was with his little daughter, and he smiled at her delight and interest in the Pifferari.

'I wonder what sort of Presepio they will have here,' said her father as he pushed open the church door and held aside the heavy curtain to let his little girl pass inside. The church was lighted only at one end by large candles, which threw their light upon the Presepio, or representation of the Holy Family at the time of our Saviour's birth. There large waxen figures were arranged: Joseph, Mary and the Babe in the Manger, and the shepherds kneeling down before him in adoration. Behind were the animals, a cow and an ass. The dim light gave all an air of reality, and Crezina gazed in rapt admiration at the scene, while the Marchese bent down and reminded her of the story of the birth of Jesus Christ.

Shortly afterwards the priests entered and the evening service began. Crezina sat quietly beside her father while he knelt and prayed. Presently the sound of weeping made her look round and she saw, not far from them, the young Pifferari who had interested her so much. He knelt on the stones and clasped his hands and raised them in entreaty towards the altar.

Crezina wondered what his grief could be, and longed to tell her father who she felt certain would be able to comfort him.

At last, the Marchese rose, and Crezina pulled his sleeve and directed his attention to the young peasant, whispering in his ear where she had seen him before and her desire to find out what his trouble was. Her father looked at the boy interestedly, then nodded, and going up to him touched his shoulder and beckoned him to go to the back of the church which was nearly empty by this time, the service being over. Only a small crowd had collected before the Presepio, mothers pointing out to their little ones the different figures and explaining the scene.

In answer to the Marchese's enquiries, Giovanni told him that he was in great distress about his mother who had been ill for some time, and was now so weak he feared she was dying: and he had no means of getting a doctor to see her.

'I have an old friend who is a doctor. Give me your address and I will request he go and see your mother tomorrow morning.'

'*Mille grazie Signor mio!*' exclaimed the lad, kissing the hand of the kind gentleman, 'May God reward you.' He then gave him the name of Asunta

Ferri; they lived in a small village up in the mountain, and he said he would come the next morning to the Villa San Renato in order to show the good doctor the way up the path. He then dried his eyes and looked comforted, as he watched them walk away.

Christmas in Syria

An extract from 'Baghdad Sketches' by John Murray which relates an account of Christmas with the ancient Syrian Christians by Freya Stark

The origins of these accounts are unknown. There were three John Murrays between 1778 and 1892. The second and third Murrays published a long series of travel books and it is likely that these sketches were part of that series. The following account appears to be written in a twentieth-century style rather than a nineteenth-century one, but extensive research has not provided an explanation for this.
The Syriac and the Armenian Christians are the oldest in the world, their chants, customs and celebration having hardly changed from the earliest days of Christianity. Attending one of their services transports one back to a time of the earliest followers of the new Gospel of Jesus Christ and the sense of continuity is electric.

Najla, my landlady, and Elias the Carpenter were Syriac Christians from Diarbekr, and belonged to that part of the Sect which Rome had gathered into its fold, without altering the old customs and ritual. Near Christmas time, Najla told me they were going to read the Gospel out in the Court by a bonfire on Christmas Eve, as every family does, and would I join in the company.

I was going out that evening, and dressed a little earlier, and found the two small boys, Jusuf and Charles, waiting on my doorstep, their feelings equally divided between the splendour of my appearance in evening dress,

and the excitement of the bonfire. They took me, one by each hand, into the open court, where small lanterns were hanging among red and green paper streamers, and a heap of dry thorns stood in one corner.

'The youngest should read, but Charles only knows his ABC,' said Najla, while she handed us candles, 'so it will be Jusuf. May the Holy Words bring you all your heart's desires, o Light of my Eyes!' She kissed me, and after her the two children came up and shyly lifted their faces to be kissed, while Elias with the tarbush pushed back off his fine old aquiline grizzled face, smiled upon us all.

Then Jusuf, who is ten, read out the Gospel, standing very straight with the lighted candle in his hand, his face full of seriousness, an impressive little figure under the stars. There was no wind; the candle flames burned clear and still. The four walls of the court shut out everything except the motionless tops of the palm trees in surrounding groves. The outer gate was locked and barred, in memory, no doubt, of many persecutions. In the childish Arabic, the old story came with a new and homely grace; and we listened, moved and silent, standing like living altars, holding our lighted candles. Then Elias bent down with a light to the fire; the children clutched my arm with excitement, 'Watch how it burns!' said Najla; for the luck of the house depends on it. The light went out.

Elias tried again – a little flame flickered and hesitated; Najla, resourceful, denied the tenets of predestination and poured paraffin on the strategic point; and the fire leapt to a blaze. It lit the children's oval faces with their long dark lashes, and Najla's long plaits with kerchief tied above them. The four voices joined in some old native psalm; and the flame of the fire rising so straight into the quiet sky made one think of yet earlier worships, of Abel and Abraham and Isaac; and older than these, for presently, Najla took my hand and made me leap thrice across them, wishing my wish, as no doubt the Babylonian maidens did to the honour of their gods.

Next morning at 4.30, when the minarets across the water scarce showed against the faintness of the dawn, my hostess and I were already on our way to Mass in the Syriac Church. The bridge of boats was deserted. The sentry, evidently a Christian also, gave poor Najla a palpitation by informing us that we should be late. Najla keeps her high heels and her walking for great occasions only, and they were a little unmanageable.

We reached the Christian quarter across the early silence of New Street, and entered the dark alleys filled with streams of quiet people on their way to the Chaldean, Armenian, Latin, Syriac or Jacobite churches, which are all hidden away unobtrusively among the labyrinth of houses. They are modern and ugly when seen in the vacant light of day, but now as we came from the half light outside, we opened the heavy door on what looked like a bed of tulips brilliantly illuminated, so vivid and rustling and shimmering were the many coloured silk izars of the women who filled the nave in the light of lamps and candles.

In the centre of the church, half hidden from the crowd, the Bishop and his clergy were busy over another bonfire, surrounded by men who chanted a swift Syriac hymn – the tongue in which legend says that Adam lamented over the death of Abel. The male congregation at the back kept up the humming monotone accompaniment which takes the place of an organ.

As we entered, the dry wood caught fire, and a sheet of flame rose halfway to the ceiling. The silken hoods round us rustled like a field of barley in the breeze. The Bishop, in a robe of cream and gold and crimson, his mitre high above the congregation, took in his arms a figure of the Infant Christ on a crimson cushion. Followed by his train, he walked slowly round the church, while a low canticle, wild no longer, but deep and grave and very touching, rose from all sides where the men were standing. The women did not sing.

After this the service continued very like a Roman Catholic High Mass. The warmth, the unknown speech, the murmur of prayer, cast a rich drowsiness over me. The Bishop's gold shoes and crimson stockings; the embroidered crimson kerchief which hung from his wrist to the ground; his long auburn beard; the silk gauntlets, coloured like blood with the Stigmata embroidered upon them in silk; the acolytes who held tall feather fans with tinkling ornaments upon them, all grew blurred in a dream. The Elevation awoke me; the bell rang, cymbals clashed, acolytes shook their fans till the ornaments rattled like dice boxes, and the rustle of the izars as the women rose to kneel was like a wave breaking softly.

Then the Bishop, bending over the altar rail, gave with his two joined hands, the touch of Peace to members of the congregation, who passed it on to the next, and so on from worshipper to worshipper, row after row, through the whole length of the church.

Soon after that Mass was over. We crushed our way out into the narrow lane, and discovered that little Charles was lost. There was a hectic search, for the sense of danger is so inbred in the Eastern Christian that it enters in a surprising way into the least threatening moments of his life. But Charles was merely lost in his own meditations behind a pillar. He woke to the ordinary facts of life when we stopped at the pastrycook's door to choose the Christmas Cakes.

The Chinese Nativity Pictures Mystery

Mainland China is strictly Communist and those who manage to practise any religion are mainly Buddhist. Any overtly embraced Christianity is confined to Hong Kong. Yet in the seventeenth century Jesuit missionaries converted people in China to Christianity as elsewhere, and there are some beautiful images of the infant Jesus in ivory mangers which look like like four-poster beds, hung with silks and silver and gold votive lamps, from those early days of the Jesuits' influence.

But this little story is from a century later and remains a mystery. Before the Second World War a bundle of photographs was sent from Peking to a small Christian propaganda publisher in London. The legend they bore stated that they were the work of different artists and were all painted in the eighteenth and early nineteenth century on silk. The legend also said that a non-Christian was commissioned to paint a series and was converted by his study of Christ's life.

An eighteenth-century Chinese silk painting of the Annunciation.

The legend and the pictures were reproduced by the Society for the Propagation of the Faith, as a testimony to these beautiful paintings. The book describes them thus:

Nearly every picture includes a tree, very often the bamboo so character-istic of China, and those which have no tree are noticeably more Western in design. It is probable that these were painted by artists who were pupils of monks from the West. The richness of details will repay closer study. Christ is generally shown in the surroundings of well-to-do Chinese life, for many artists would feel it irreverent to portray Christ in poverty.

This tells of a distinct difference in the perception of the Christmas story for these early Christian converts. Westerners accept that Jesus was born lowly.

The originals are believed to be in churches scattered throughout China or in private homes. The publishers of the little book of pictures could not trace them and in 1984 the author attempted to do so. But even with the help of the Chinese Embassy, this proved impossible, so they must forever remain a mystery.

Within a Lodge of Broken Bark

CHRISTMAS BROUGHT TO THE HURON INDIANS IN CANADA

John P. Robarts and others

Canada's first Christmas carol was cradled in Huronia, the pleasant land that circles the south-eastern shores of Georgian Bay. According to tradition, it was written by a Jesuit missionary, Father Jean de Brébeuf, to interpret the Nativity story to the Huron Indians. It was contained in a manuscript left by his fellow priest, Father Pierre-Joseph Chaumonot, at Lorette near Quebec, where the Christian Hurons finally settled after the dispersion of their nation in 1649–50.

His exceptional talent for languages led him to translate many Christian truths into Huron and this well-loved Christmas story, sung in the pleasant, undulating tones of the native tongue, must have given him and his fellow missionaries special delight. Often it must have been heard at Sainte-Marie among the Hurons, home of the Jesuits deep in the forests of Huronia, over 800 miles from the small French posts on the St Lawrence River.

Father Brébeuf used to call himself an ox, after his name, humbly claiming that he was only fit to carry loads, so one wonders how he became a scholarly Jesuit instead of a Franciscan whose order would have been blessed by Father Jean's particular humility.

He went to Canada some time after 1615 as superior of the Huron mission, learning their language and their respect. In a letter sent back to his seminary in Rouen, he described the Huron celebration of Christmas. 'The Indians have a particular devotion for the night that was enlightened by the birth of the Son of God. They built a small chapel of cedar and fir branches in honour of the manger of the Infant Jesus. . . . Even those who were a distance of two day's journey met at a given place to sing hymns in honour of the new-born Child.'

Father Brébeuf told the Christmas story in a way that the Indians could relate to. The angel choirs appeared to the braves, the stable became a bark lodge and chiefs from afar worshipped at the manger of the Infant King, who was dressed in rabbit skins.

Originally written in about 1641, it was lost and not re-written down until the late eighteenth century, when another missionary heard the Indians singing the carol, and wrote the words down there and then in the original Huron. He had to invent a symbol (like a figure of eight) for a strange 'ou' sound. A few lines of that old carol follows:

> Estennialon de tson8e Jes8s ahatonhia
> Onna8ate8a d'oki n'on8andask8aentak.

The following verses are taken from an interpretation of the original by one Mr Middleton from the early years of this century, and given to me by the government of the Province of Ontario.

'Twas in the moon of winter time when all the birds had fled,
That Mighty Gitchi Manitou sent angel choirs instead
Before their light the stars grew dim
And wandering hunters heard the hymn:
Jesus, your King is born
Jesus is born
In excelsis gloria!

Within a lodge of broken bark the tender babe was found
A ragged robe of rabbit skin wrapped his beauty 'round.
And as the hunter braves drew nigh,
The angel song grew loud and high:
CHORUS

The illustration by Stanley Turner of the Huronia Christmas carol, 1927. Courtesy of the Huronia Historical Development Council.

The earliest moon of winter time is not so round and fair
As was the ring of glory on the helpless infant there.
While chiefs from far before him knelt
With gifts of Fox and Beaver pelt
CHORUS

You children of the forest free, O sons of Manitou
The Holy Child of earth and heav'n is born today for you
Come kneel before the radiant Boy
Who brings you beauty, peace and joy.
CHORUS

The custom persisted among the Indians to dress as Kings and coming in procession, singing their carols, bringing gifts to their chief, in memory of the Magi bringing gifts to the King of Peace on that Christmas night long ago.

The Putz

CHRISTMAS IN THE COMMUNITY OF THE FIRST MORAVIAN CHURCH, BETHLEHEM, PENNSYLVANIA, USA

Lee Butterfield of the Putz Committee

Ours is such a special Christmas, we are happy to share it with others. The putz is the most noted of our special Christmas customs. But besides there is music – concerts, carollers, choirs, singing the Christmas portion of the Messiah, and the like.

There also are the candle services at which everyone is given a lighted beeswax taper which has a red ruffle at its base, and by its light the last hymns of the service are sung. The red of the paper ruffle is a reminder of the Saviour's sacrifice while the lighted candle reminds us of the Light of the World and the warmth of His Love.

Two more customs – the many-pointed Moravian Star which is made in many sizes, from a little one that hangs on the Christmas tree to the big one, about 6 feet across, that is hung in Central Church at Advent. These are made of translucent paper or plastic now, so that a light bulb can be suspended inside. Many people hang medium-sized stars in their doorways for a Christmas decoration. Many people also put candles in their windows, electric ones for safety but a very welcoming sight. Another delightful custom is making very thin crisp cookies cut out in shapes such as stars and chickens and trees and whatever interesting shapes the cookie cutter maker can devise.

The putz was a family decoration and during Christmas week there was much visiting around to appreciate the variety and imagination each family put into theirs. Many families still have them as their main Christmas decoration, but so many outsiders coming to town to see them became a problem! This led to Central's members making a public putz. The word putz is an archaic use of a German word meaning 'to decorate'.

Each year it is built anew, these days in the Christian Education building. In November we go to the hills for moss to make the green fields for the sheep and the shepherds. Small evergreen trees are cut to make the background. On Thanksgiving week-end all the stored materials are carried out, the platform put together, and the work begins. The platform makes a table about 12 x 14 foot, and about 2 foot above the ground. Large empty cans are filled with wet sand to make bases for the trees. A roll of blue cloth arches over the platform, making a sky. Boxes and boards are arranged to make a hilly terrain when covered with crumpled wet newspaper over which are put the large pieces of moss. Top centre is the Holy Family. Other scenes are arranged around this central piece. Lights are arranged for each scene.

Someone recites the Christmas story, beginning with some of the prophecies of Isaiah, and the lights are lit to show each appropriate scene in the accounts of Luke and Matthew.

Bethlehem was founded in 1741 to be a centre of evangelism especially to the Indians and settlers without a church. It was named on Christmas Eve, 1741 in a very moving service. This was the beginning of our Christmas tradition. Bethlehem began as a planned community, with everyone working to support those who went out as teachers and preachers. For many years, only members of the Moravian Church could live here. Everyone contributed their day's labour in return for which they had their food, clothing, shelter, medical treatment when needed; their children were taught, they had some say in the government. Meanwhile the town grew from one five-storey log house to a series of large stone buildings and a reputation for having good products and able craftsmen, cheerful, hospitable residents and much religious music.

Swinging Lanterns as We Go in Belgium

This short account was dictated by an elderly lady who had been a governess in Belgium before the First World War. Her dates were vague, but her memories were like sharp pictures and her face lit up with the tales.

Belgium has always been famous for its living crèche tableaux. These are scenes of the Nativity at the stable of Bethlehem, but, instead of statues, they are real people and animals. They sit for an hour or more in town squares and suchlike, while carols are sung and prayers read. The most famous are from Liège, Brugge, Brussels and Ghent, but they are as popular throughout Walloon and Flemish Belgium. When we went to Liège, there were several stalls set up around the square, selling little crèche figures, and food and drink. The most popular were the little pancakes which were called 'bouquettes', delicious served hot in a twist of paper to catch the oil in which they were cooked.

Sometimes these are still tableaux, other times they are acted out. There are other types of play too. Once, while visiting relatives of the family I worked for, we were taken to see the marionette play in the famous wool town of Verviers. This took place in the town hall, I think. It was a huge building, anyway, with trestle tables covered in floor-length cloths. The different scenes of the '*vita*' of Jesus was enacted on each trestle. The puppets were moved by rods which went through the table tops and were done by children who sat under the tables, hidden from view by the cloths.

The story is told by an old woman puppet, who points to each scene with a stick. It is traditional for the peasants, the shepherds and suchlike to speak in Walloon dialect, which I could not understand and there was much whispering as my children and many other people explained to the 'foreign' visitors from outside the region what was being said, for the famous event attracted thousands of visitors. There were many other such plays all over the Walloon district, but this was the best it was said. In contrast, the Virgin Mary spoke in the purest French, in respect for her status!

One year we were taken by the Master to Kortrijk, where they had a special procession of the Three Kings and enormous bonfires were lit around the town. I never understood. It was my first Christmas there, and things were still a little strange, especially as I was heartily homesick for my own family and wondering what they were doing at home and if they felt as miserable without my presence as I did so far away from them at this time of year when everyone should be with their dear ones. So, I did not really take in what was going on, though the family were being very kind in taking me all that way to see the spectacle.

It was also possible to buy a sort of white pudding at the markets, which was then served as part of the Christmas dinner. This was a little like the Scottish savoury white pudding, and probably had some kind of oatmeal or suchlike in it, but I never liked to ask. We also had hare, or maybe rabbit. Very different to the English Christmas dinner!

We used to go to midnight mass always. Across the fields often in the snow, or deep hard frost, and swinging our lanterns as we went, the light sparkled on the frosty ground. We would meet up with others coming, farmers, and all their families, mothers with babes bundled up against the cold night. Nobility too, finding it better to walk the short distance across the fields than to risk the horses' feet on the hard cobbles and ruts of

A lantern party from the early years of the twentieth century.

79

the long roadway. There was something very special in all meeting up like that, a sense of continuity of hundreds of years of Christmas worshippers. The Noels, special ancient carols which were sung, had been sung the same for hundreds of years. For our church was old enough to have seen nearly a thousand years of Christmas worship. Now of course, they go by car – customs change.

As we went we would chatter. The grown-ups would tell the age-old stories, not only of the mystery of the Holy Night, but of the many legends and folk tales which had grown up around the villages. For example, the sheep are said to turn to the East on Christmas Eve, in remembrance of that night on the hill above Bethlehem, when the great Star appeared to the shepherds. Cows and other beasts kneel in their stables on the stroke of midnight, as if in adoration of the Birth of Jesus, and all the bees come out of their hives, and hum! Of course no one knows if this is true, as we are all in adoration ourselves at that particular hour!

We governesses would, like the farmers' wives, eagerly read the local papers to see what story had been printed for Christmas Eve, to tell the children on the way to church. It is a custom which I believe still exists – or it did up to a few years ago anyway, because I still used to subscribe to the papers – and a good one too, because it keeps the old stories and traditions alive.

St Lucy and the Legend of the Lady of Varmland

from Giftbringers of the World

Lucy was a saint in the early Church who was martyred for her faith. Although her eyes were put out, she miraculously could still see, and so she was put to death. Her name means 'Light' and signifies that fact that she was blind yet saw. While she lived she was known to distribute bread to the poor, and after her death the story of her charity and her miraculous sight became intermingled into the legend which travelled through Byzantium and later northwards up the eastern rivers and up through Europe with the Viking incursions.

From early times there had existed in Varmland in Western Sweden a legend of a young woman who appeared out of nowhere in a huge ship which sailed around a lake. The lady was surrounded by a light and her ship was laden with food, which she distributed to the starving people.

Was this person perhaps a Celtic goddess the memory of whom was left there from pre-Christian times; whose story became mingled with that of Lucia whose story travelled northwards on the trade routes from Byzantium? Lucia did, after all, come from Syracuse in Sicily. There was a Celtic tribe in this part of Western Sweden, and the story would connect with the Welsh legend of the Lady of the Lake who came out of the mist on a food-laden ship. Sounds almost the same story, doesn't it?

Today the Lucia legend merges with the Varmland legend, having been brought by eleventh-century missionaries to the other areas of Sweden. But the fact is that the legend began only in the Varmland area and has only spread within the last hundred years or so. So something of a mystery remains.

A well researched but so far unproven theory to the solution of this mystery is that a trading ship from Byzantium found its way to the famine stricken people of Western Sweden, and provided them with much needed supplies. On these same ships came the stories of the martyr Lucia 'whose eyes were blind but she saw with the light of God'. Over the centuries, the story of the famine and the aid ship, the story of the Sicilian martyr Lucia and the older legend of the Lady of the Lake mingled together. The event was commemorated there-after by the 'appearance' of a

The mysterious legendary Lady of Varmland, from an original painting by Patricia Fallace for Christmas Archives.

young woman with lights around her, wearing the white robes of a Virgin and the red sash of a martyr, and gradually became the Lucyfest the Swedes know today.

Lucy appears throughout Sweden both communally and within the family. In each home the youngest daughter is dressed in the white robe and red sash, and has a wreath with nine candles on her head. She awakens the family with coffee and 'Lussekatte', which are a sweetdough bun with a special scroll design, which shape may have come from a more ancient custom, and intended to represent the Sun. Some theories say that the shape is a relic of the original bread brought by the ship so long ago. Many places in the Mediterranean countries still have cakes of similar shapes today, said to have had some religious significance long forgotten, especially in Sicily, whose cuisine is most ancient. The mingling of customs is not ignored here because the rituals of the old solstice included many fires to light up the darkness in a country where only four hours' daylight existed in midwinter. Similar customs existed in Sicily where Lucia was born, and obviously bear more relation to the pagan rituals than to the saint.

POPULAR TRADITIONS

Silent Night – the True Tale of Austria's Most Famous Carol

Austria, positioned as it is in Central Europe, is steeped in the customs and folklore of both East and West. It was part of the Austro-Hungarian Empire and the Ottoman Empire. It has borders with Italy, Germany and Switzerland, which add to the colourful tapestry of year-round celebration. Unlike many other countries, Austria has not abandoned the

processions, dancing and thanksgiving for Easter, Whitsuntide, Corpus Christi, etc. and other festivals.

Christmas is no exception and the variety of traditions associated with the feast are widely contrasting. Here you will find the evening procession of the Crib makers, who ski by flaming torches from village to village with their Christmas cribs; and the calm beauty of the Silent Night Chapel in Oberndorf; and the moving and solemn services held in the Hof-Capel in Innsbruck contrasting with the Christmas crib in the Carolino Augusteum Museum in Salzburg. Every figure featured bears the face of Richard Meyer, an eccentric opera singer who created the crib in his own likeness. Another very ancient and colourful tradition is the Perchtenlauf, *the Tyrolean* Perchtenfest *which has its roots back in pre-Christian times. The* Perchten *are descendants of the old* Frauen, *the female deities of the alpine regions of Central Europe who each had specific characteristics, but these have become intertwined and muddled over the centuries. Now the* Perchten *are represented by ancient carved masks depicting grotesque animals and witches which are passed on from father to son. Wearing the masks, the men run through the streets and join a wild parade to 'Scare the Winter away'.*

And one should not forget the grand New Year balls and concerts, the 'Silvester Programmes', with the Vienna State Orchestra playing the music of the Strauss family, and televised throughout the world. With such a wealth of tradition it has been difficult to decide which elements to include in this section on Austrian Christmas, but while doing some research in Austria in 1985, a man approached and introduced himself as 'Egon'. He said that his story was the true story of the most loved carol in the world, 'Silent Night'. The story had come down through his own family, from father to son, and he had

Perchtenfest *mask.*

spent many years tracing the truth of it, and he hoped it would be published. Loath to accept anything so important on one encounter, we searched high and low, but could find little to substantiate his story. However, it is included here as a most interesting tale which could well be true!

'Everyone today says that Franz Gruber wrote the tune to 'Silent Night' on Christmas Eve 1818, when the church organ broke down, while Josef Mohr wrote the words. That is only partly true. Let me tell you the true story.'

'Herr Gruber was a music teacher – he taught my great-great-grandfather. He was good and he knew all the old folk tunes from the hills round about. He wrote the tune based on an old folk song.

'But Pastor Mohr had composed words for a carol some time earlier. He only came to Oberndorf in 1817, but had written the verse long before he arrived. The pictures of him are wrong too – they show him as an old man. He was made a priest in 1815 and I believe that he wrote the poem the Christmas following his ordination. The story everyone tells is that he wrote the carol on the way home from visiting a parishioner at Oberndorf. Well, maybe he did write it after seeing a parishioner, I don't know that, but it certainly was not in Oberndorf, it was when he was still at Mariapfarr, and he left there sometime in 1817–18.

The chapel memorial to Fr Josef Mohr and Herr Franz Gruber.

'He showed his song to his friend, Herr Gruber, and asked him to compose a simple tune which could be used for the service on Christmas night 1818.

'Well, of course, Herr Gruber was an educated man, don't misunderstand me. But how could anyone compose a tune to fit written words so quickly, eh? He **took** an existing folk tune from up in the mountains and adapted it, adding a bit, taking a bit. It is common practice, many great composers have done so – Bartók, Kodály, Strauss! He wrote his tune around the older folk tune, I tell you!'

He paused, looking over my husband's shoulder, to make sure all the details were taken down correctly. 'You must get this right, mind', he insisted. 'Herr Gruber was a good man, a God-fearing man, he would not want to be acknowledged as a greater composer than he was!'

Here I had a number of questions – what of the story that the carol was sung by folk singers **after** that Christmas in 1818? The old man asked my husband and me to wait while he hurried back to his own house. He came back with a huge sheaf of papers and notes, which he gave to my husband. 'Keep these, read them and use them well', he entreated. It was obviously very important to him.

'Now I will answer you', he said, turning to me. 'The following year, there was enough money to have the organ repaired. It was the organ mender, Herr Mauracher, who came, heard the story of the carol and took it back to the Tyrol with him, they say. Some say that he passed the carol on to a glovemaker family called Bruder Strasser, who visited many fairs throughout Europe, passing on the story as they went, and it eventually came to the attention of the Royal Chapel in Berlin, who wrote to Herr Gruber about it.

'The story which came through my relatives was that the family of folk singers had been touring Europe, with this Tyrolean folktune in their repertoire, before 1818. That is why it caught on so well as a Christmas carol, because it was a tune which people already half knew.

'Herr Mauracher wrote down the carol and gave it (or maybe sold it) to a family of folk singers, who travelled around the Empire singing traditional songs, and thereby its fame spread. Whether they were the same folk singers I don't know. Maybe there is truth in both stories. But at one time it was even thought that Mohr wrote both verse and music, and at another time it was said that Gruber wrote both verse and music! People hear a little and interpret much.'

Two items from his sheaf of papers were interesting. One was the obituary notice of Franz Gruber, published in the Salzburger Zeitung, *which referred to the fact that the melody was 'a German folksong, and found in a few editions and collections, however always without*

*information about the poet . . . [Fr Mohr] it appearing [**the words**] to be the work of the composer'.*

The other piece was an attempt to rectify past wrongs. It is written in black script from an old newspaper, the Salzburger Chronik.

'Invited once again with other students (Franz Goichl, Johann Wachthoser) to stay with the hospitable Revd Josef Mohr in Wagrain, a blessed state of mind was fostered in us by the poet who brought "Silent Night" to life. He gave thanks and said that for him one of the most precious moments of his life was shortly before Christmas 1818, he spoke to Mr Franz Gruber about a joint effort. "The two of us did something for the Holy Night", that was how it happened. "I transcribed the words and Franz Gruber the melodie", these were always the words the Revd Mohr said.'

It is probable that, in accord with Egon's comment that one hears a little

The Krampuslauf, *a traditional Tyrolean walk of the* Krampus *and his entourage through the mountain villages.*

and invents more, this could have been the origin of the belief that the words were written at the same time as the music.
Maybe as the old man said, the story is a mix of many elements. Whichever, its simplicity appeals to the world and it has been transcribed into over forty languages worldwide, making it the most popular Christmas carol in the world.

> Silent Night! Holy Night
> All is calm, All is Bright
> Round yon Virgin, Mother and Child
> Holy Infant, so tender and mild,
> Sleep in Heavenly peace
> Sleep in Heavenly peace.

Since writing the item about the origins of 'Silent Night', the original Mohr manuscript has been found, signed and dated and authenticated. It proves that the Revd Mohr did in fact write his words in 1816, thus vindicating at least that part of Egon's story. We are grateful to Mr William Egan of the USA for his helpful advice.

Yuletide in Scotland

Edited from contributions by Margaret Ferguson and others

One thinks of Scotland as having more affinity with Hogmanay than with Christmas and, indeed, the old customs referring to Christmastide specifically are more often called 'Yule' customs, from Scotland's strong historical ties with the Norse race. An elderly Scottish neighbour of my grandmother's would threaten darkly that the 'Ashman will surely come and tak' ye awa in his sack if ye misbehave'. The strange connection between this character and the German 'Aschenklas', who was one of the frightening characters who came in St Nicholas's entourage to punish naughty children, is marked. All the Scandinavian countries believed in the

The Scottish art of curling – winter sports in Scotland, c. 1890.

'Hoardes', groups of unbaptised spirits which roamed at Christmastide. They still feature in the Christmas parades in alpine and northern regions as part of the Santa Claus/St Nicholas celebrations. It is probable that the Scottish and Northern 'Ashman' has his origins in this old belief. Margaret Ferguson found the following forfeits game, in an early nineteenth-century book of rhymes and traditions of Scotland. It appears to be a Scottish version of 'The Twelve Days of Christmas'. Forfeit games, particularly at Christmas, certainly go back to Tudor times, perhaps even further. One person would start the song and go to each in turn; when one made a mistake in the sequence, he or she had to pay a forfeit. The popular song which many know today is thought to have originated in France but, if this is true, the Scots have made it very much their own in this version.

The Yule Days

The King sent his lady on the first Yule Day
A Papingo-aye.

The King sent his lady on the second Yule Day
Two partridges and a Papingo-aye.

The King sent his lady on the third Yule Day
Three plovers, two partridges and a Papingo-aye.

The King sent his lady on the fourth Yule Day
A Goose of gray, etc.

The King sent his lady on the fifth Yule Day
Three Goldspinks, etc.

The King sent his lady on the sixth Yule Day
Three Starlings, etc.

The King sent his lady on the seventh Yule Day
A Bull that was brown, etc.

The King sent his lady on the eighth Yule Day
Three ducks a-laying, etc.

The King sent his lady on the ninth Yule Day
Three Swans a-swimming, etc.

The King sent his lady on the tenth Yule Day
A big Baboon, etc.

The King sent his lady on the eleventh Yule Day
Three Hinds a-hunting, etc.

The King sent his lady on the twelfth Yule Day
Three Maids a-dancing, etc.

The King sent his lady on the Thirteenth Yule Day
Three stalks o' corn, three maids a-dancing, three
Hinds a-hunting, a big Baboon, three Swans a-
swimming, three Ducks a-laying, a Bull that was
brown, three Starlings, three Goldspinks, a Goose
of gray, three Plovers, three Partridges, and a
Papingo-aye.

Twelfth Night, which was traditionally the time for parties and jollity, was the most popular time to play such games as the forfeits song above. In Scotland the special Twelfth Night Cake, which was sometimes baked in a pastry crust cake, became known as Black Bun. (In England it became Christmas cake.) This is a very rich very dark fruit cake, almost black with the solid fruit in it. At one time, before Christianity came to British shores, cakes were made as sacramentals. Scottish cakes adopted from Viking times often had a sun shape, like the traditional Scottish shortbread, which is also popular at Yuletide. With Christianity came the symbolic quartering of cakes to represent the Cross. Although most Yule breads and shortcakes are now baked in the oven, at one time the were placed on a girdle, an iron sheet or even a hot flat stone, over a fire. In Shetland they still eat 'Yule-brunnies' which, until recently, often had a hole in the centre and rays marked around the edge to represent the sun's rays.

The bannock is not so far removed from this and probably had the same origin. A recipe book in 1879 describes the Hogmanay bannock as a flat cake made with fresh ground oatmeal flavoured with caraway seeds. Round, flat, with a hole in the middle and nipped around the edge. Great care had to be taken not to break the bannock in the making as this would bring bad luck. Cooked on a bakestone on top of the fire, these cakes were sent all over the world, particularly to those who had settled in New World countries – America, Canada, Australia and New Zealand – by their families back home in Scotland.

A Chinese Christmas Without Customs

Various contributors

*In searching for the Chinese Christmas I found many contradictions.
Perhaps it is best described by the following quote from Herbert
Wernecke's book, which relates to the comments of a missionary to
China who told the following story about a dinner in Pennsylvania in
the 1930s:*

Last Christmas Season the Cosmopolitan Club at State College
Pennsylvania held a very interesting meeting at which a representative
from every country whose natives were present was requested to tell of
the Christmas customs of his country. The Chinese student who
responded said that the Chinese people do not have Christmas, and so
have no Christmas customs; then he told at length about the New Year
customs of his people. . . .

The Chinese people have no Christmas! Yet in small pockets where the
missionaries persisted into the early years of the twentieth century there
are customs and observances to be found. They even have a Santa Claus
figure, who is called Dun che Lao Ren ('Christmas Old Man'), and
children hang up their stocking for his visit as they do all over the world.
Christmas gifts are exchanged and have a strict code. Fine items, such as
costly jewellery, silken garments, expensive fancy goods, are only given to
members of the immediate family, whereas small gifts, such as food,
flowers, scent sachets, tassels, etc. are given to distant friends and relatives.
In some Christianized pockets there is a Christmas Eve Lantern parade,
which is very beautiful, with dozens of hand-painted colourful paper
lanterns lit with candlelights and held on a bamboo frame.

*The following account is from a mission teacher at the turn of the
twentieth century:*

Christmas Day in Far Cathay by the Revd Lloyd, Fuh-Chow, China

It is Christmas Morning in far off China. There is yet no sign of the coming dawn, no shaft of light piercing the Eastern horizon, but suddenly out of the darkness arises the sound of the old familiar hymn of our childhood, sung by Chinese voices to the same old tune, 'While Shepherds Watched'. Then after a brief pause, 'Hark the Herald Angels' rings through the air.

We who until thus awakened have been sound asleep, gradually recover our senses and realize that the schoolboys have come to remind us that the Anniversary of the 'Great Birthday' has arrived . . . Soon the sun peeps over the Kushan mountain and we are ready to go to the College Chapel for our Chinese Christmas service. As we approach the building we see that it has been rather elaborately decorated for the occasion by the students. Outside, Chinese and Japanese lanterns of various designs are hanging from the walls, and large gilt-lettered texts remind us that He whose birth as a little baby we are remembering to-day is also the Mighty God, the Everlasting Father, and the Prince of Peace. Inside the chief incidents of the first Christmastide are depicted for us by Chinese artists. Their ideas are

Chinese carol-singers at the Fuh-Chow Mission, 1900.

somewhat hazy as to some of the objects which they endeavour to make visible by means of cotton wool and Chinese paper, and the results of their artistic efforts are sometimes rather grotesque.

One tableau represents the interview of the angels with the shepherds, and we notice specially the interesting attitude of the sheep, and the very large Eastern Star shining in solitary splendour above the scene. The Wise Men are in a revolving lantern, and at the present moment, as the lantern is unlighted, we may see them actually wending their way, perched on camels, to that rude cradle at Bethlehem, the boxes containing their offerings carefully strapped on in front of them. . . .

At the Headquarters of the CEZMS in Fuh-Chow, there is a Christmas tree loaded with useful gifts, made by busy workers in England, Ireland and Australia. As individual names are called out by the willing helpers, eager hands are stretched out towards them, and shrill voices say, 'Chu wai, chu wai', 'here, here'. Gradually the tree is lightened of its load . . . dolls affording the greatest pleasure to the little girls from the Blind school.

Finland – A Winter Fairyland

Kaisu Vuolio and others

Christmas in Finland is very like Christmas in England used to be until religious practice was abandoned and overwork and sophistication took the 'spirit' away! It is impossible to paint an accurate picture of a Finnish Christmas briefly, so a few special elements have been chosen to best represent this most Christmassy country: the *Pikkijoulu* – 'Little Christmas' – the sauna, the tree, the graveyards and of course, the real Father Christmas who resides at Rovaneimi – and those who can afford it can pay a luxurious visit to Santaland via Concorde.

It has sometimes been said that northern people appreciate Christmas the most, and this does seem to be true. After the long, dark and often very wet autumn, Christmas marks the turning of the year. Light begins to win over darkness. It's time to celebrate. Preparing for the year's biggest festival also makes the autumn go faster!

Christmas is not just two days, it is preceded by a lengthy and cheerful period of busy preparation. For the Church Christmas begins with the first Sunday of Advent, but long before this, as early as October, countless associations have already set about planning their Christmas bazaars. Members get together in the old Finnish tradition, most often to make Christmas decorations. These evening gatherings could also be regarded as the first Christmas parties, called by the delightful name of *Pikkijoulu*, meaning 'Little Christmas', since they always include some type of Christmas programme, talks, music and special seasonal delicacies.

The *Pikkijoulu* has been part of the Finnish tradition since the 1920s, and every employer of any size arranges one for their staff. Every organization throws a party too. Even town councils may forget their political differences and join forces for one happy evening. They may put on a play or sketch for the amusement of their staff.

The first Sunday of Advent officially opens the Christmas season, the Church resounding with the strains of Vogler's 'Hosanna'. All people flock to hear it. All over the country there are advent concerts in the evening.

It is around this time that the Christmas lights come on in the shops and offices. The centres of towns are full of light. Pietarsaari, a town on the west coast, has had a Christmas Street ever since the 1840s. Suspended over the street are three giant decorations: a cross symbolizing faith; an anchor representing hope; and a heart, the symbol of love. In the olden days they were lit with candles; nowadays the candles are electric. Only war, the start of the oil crisis, and the introduction of an outdoor Christmas tree have temporarily interrupted their use.

The Finnish Christmas tree usually has flags of many nations on it as a reminder of friendship among people, and straw items – intricate shapes which are made carefully by families, using straw which has been softened by the heated steam from the sauna! One family told the story that they have a sauna party, and take lots of straw into the sauna. The whole family participates. There they spend the time chatting and making ornaments for their tree: geometrical shapes, St Andrew's crosses and Stars, and also little goats, representing the 'Yulebok', a mythical creature who comes through the town at night.

The sauna is an integral part of the Finnish Christmas. Even in the early years of the twentieth century, people were expected to 'attend' the sauna on Christmas Eve afternoon. And still today, anyone travelling around the Finnish countryside will see smoke rising from almost every sauna house.

Christmas Eve is the highlight of the year in Finland, and not Christmas Day. Families get together for the occasion, and children who have grown up and moved away from home will try to be with their families for the holidays. It is still a working day; however the shops are open only until mid-day, providing one last chance to buy those last few gifts and dainties for the table. At precisely 12 noon the 'Peace of Christmas' is proclaimed in Turku, the former capital of Finland, along with advices and greetings dating back to the Middle Ages. Most Finns listen to this ceremony on the radio, and it marks the beginning of the Feast.

At sunset, families make their way to the churchyard where a service is often held at 5 o'clock. Candles are placed on the graves of loved ones, sometimes possibly a wreath. A Finnish graveyard is a breathtaking sight on Christmas Eve. Thousands of candles shining out across the snow are a sight no foreigner will forget. In many towns former soldiers will go in procession

The Finnish Father Christmas, or Youlupukki. *Finnish Tourist Board.*

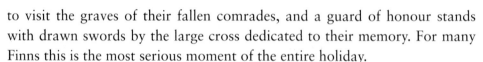
to visit the graves of their fallen comrades, and a guard of honour stands with drawn swords by the large cross dedicated to their memory. For many Finns this is the most serious moment of the entire holiday.

Back at home the excitement mounts as the family awaits a quite different aspect of Christmas: the arrival of Father Christmas. The Finnish Father Christmas, originally called *Youlupukki*, lives in Korvantunturi, Finnish Lapland, a hill situated on Finland's Eastern border at Savukoski. The top of the 483-metre high hill is in three peaks, and the international border runs right through it.

Finland differs from other countries in that Father Christmas really does come to the house in person on Christmas Eve. When he arrives he always asks, 'Are there any good children here?' and the answer is always an enthusiastic, 'YES'. He generally brings a large basket containing all the presents. Then the children sing to him before he distributes the gifts after which he tramps off into the snowy night to visit the other houses.

Christmas is a festival centred on the family and particularly the children. It is the season to recall what tends to be forgotten the rest of the year but which is nevertheless important: other people, roots and traditions and the idea of peace on earth and goodwill to all men.

The Norwegian Birds' Christmas Dinner

An extract from Christmas in Norway by Vera Henriksen

To the group of Grain Sheaves traditions in Norway belongs the sheaf of oats which a great number of Norwegian families still faithfully erect each Christmas for the enjoyment of the birds; this sheaf with the many-hued birds is a favourite subject with designers of Norwegian Christmas cards.

Putting up the Sheaf of Corn for the Birds' Christmas meal in Norway, from a nineteenth-century illustration. Courtesy of the Norwegian Folk Museum.

Theories regarding the origin of the *julenek* Christmas sheaf vary; there is agreement only that its original purpose certainly was not to please the birds.

Some authorities are of the opinion that it once was a sacrifice to fertility deities; others think it has been a 'magic' means to keep the birds from damaging next year's crops. One can take one's pick of these theories.

The custom in some districts of using the first sheaf of the harvest for the purpose indicates some kind of sacrifice. It is a universal custom that the first sheaf should be sacrificed. But in other places, the last sheaf, or straws gathered from the fields after the harvest, is used, and this supports the theory of magic.

The Polish Szopka

The form of the Polish crib is varied; in the mountains they are carved with relief pictures, showing the shepherds dressed in traditional garb for example. But in Krakow they have a special tradition. It is a Nativity scene set inside the doors of a model of the Wawel Cathedral. Every year there is a competition to find the best model. People come from all over Poland, not just Krakow. The cribs can be 6 inches high, or 6 feet. Some have mechanisms, or lights. There are two elements which are the same – they all are covered in coloured foils, and they all have the same architectural structure as the cathedral.

This competition began in 1937. It was intended to bring back to life a tradition which had died shortly after the First World War, that of the crib theatre. To the square in Krakow's centre come the artists carrying their Szopka. It is a magnificent sight. The winners are kept in the Museum of Ethnography; the rest are sold in a gloriously colourful market place, overlooked by the statue of Poland's famous author, Adam Mickiewicz. The best ones are snapped up as quickly as they are put down. The event is covered by world reporters and has become probably the most famous Christmas tradition of modern Poland.

Abrozy Grabowski, eminent Polish historian, recorded in 1831 one of the most complete descriptions of the origin of the Szopka. From him we learn just what it was that the Poles of Krakow wished to preserve with the start of the competition in 1937. He wrote:

A Szopka is a small itinerant theatre made up of coloured paper, which boys are taking round households to the amusement of children each evening, starting with Christmas Eve and till Candlemas Day, that is to say, throughout January. The actors in the crib are dolls (puppets), which one of the boys, kneeling behind the crib, sets in motion, carrying the suitable dialogue and singing various concepts. The main parts are: King Herod with the Jew beside him, a Cracovian and his bride, a mountaineer and his woman, a Cossack, peasants and their steward, a Jew and Jewish woman who, all in pairs, leave the crib and

The beautiful traditional Christmas crib peculiar to Krakow, the Szopka.

The Christmas market outside the Wawel Cathedral in Krakow's town square, c. 1930.

dance and sing in front of it. A soldier also comes out and disperses the dancing dolls.

This portable puppet theatre was common throughout Poland in earlier times, and in common with similar practice in Hungary, was accompanied by Starboys who sang carols. It was in 1808 that the Krakow Szopka in the style of a church rather than a theatre, which may have been an earlier style or even a different style which was around at the same time, was eloquently recorded. In the diary of Kazimierz Girtler is written:

It was for the first time too that I could see a crib, only it was not the kind of civilized crib which imitates the theatre but an old-time dressed up stable, with the Holy Child, Holy Virgin, St Joseph, kings and shepherds as well as an ox and a donkey. On either side of the stable there are two towers as if the said stable was put up in a chapel. Candlelit windows of the towers cast a glamour around. The drama consisted of the arrival of the three kings followed by the shepherds and then the action developed, helped along by the dextrous hands of a boy who, sitting behind the crib, directed the movements of these puppets on sticks. A chorus sang carol songs from canticles instead of speeches and conversation from the figures on the stage.

Dancing to the Goigs in Catalonia

*Singing and dancing forms a very important part of Spanish Christmas. The
Sevillians have the Dance of Sixes, which is an intricate dance performed as
part of the start of the Christmas ceremonies outside Seville Cathedral.
Another cathedral to bear witness to the religious dances is the Sagrada
Familia in Barcelona. Every Sunday in fact, the Catalans dance the
Sardanas. Only a true Catalan can dance without counting the intricate
steps – you can hear the muttering of those not familiar with the Sardanas
counting their steps. At Christmas they dance it to the Goigs. These are
Songs of Joy, long songs which describe Bible stories, and the Christmas
story in particular, in a simple way which describes the land of Catalonia as
much as the story. One in particular tells of the lovely things which come
out of Catalonia – there is the grape and the raisin, the fig, the almond
and the olive, flowers, cheeses, honey and the last verse is of course
he Goig.*

*One of the most famous Christmas Goigs is 'The Carol of the Birds'. This
Goig dates from the seventeenth century and originally contained fourteen
verses describing the visit of thirty-two birds to the Christchild. The eagle, the
sparrow, the finch, thrush, robin and lark all sing their lovely best; even the
harsh voices of the magpie, jay, cuckoo, raven and fat little partridge are not
left out.*

*When I was in Spain, I had the great pleasure of hearing the superb Catalan cellist
Pablo Casals play. Whether it was Christmas or not, his signature tune was 'The
Carol of the Birds'. The cadence and fall of the notes really do bring to mind the
picture of the birds fluttering and flying around the stable. Casals said, 'I began the
custom of concluding my concerts with the melody of the old Catalan Carol, the
"Song of the Birds". It tells a tale of the Nativity; how beautiful and tender is that
tale, with its reverence for life and for man, the noblest expression of life! In the
Catalan Carol, it is the eagle and the sparrows, the nightingales and the little wrens
who sing a welcome to the Infant, singing of him as a flower that will delight the
earth with its sweet scent.'*

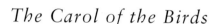

The Carol of the Birds

A Star rose in the sky
And gave a great light
In that splendid night.
The Birds sweetly sang
To carol and rejoice
And they came with pretty voices.

The Eagle left his nest
And rose up in the air
To sing this melody.
He sang, Jesus is born
To release us from sin
And give us happiness.

The Sparrow then resounds
This night is Christmas Night
A night of great contentment.
The Robin and the Finch
Together, sang as well
Oh, what a happy feeling!

And then the Lark enjoined
This is not wintertime
But it must be springtime.
For now has been born a flower
Which gives out fragrance pure
On earth and in heaven too.

The Magpie, Thrush and Jay
They answered, This is May
Responding to our yearnings.
Now all the trees are green
And all the plants flower
As if it were springtime.

And then sang the Cuckoo
You birds, all come, all come
To celebrate the dawn.
And the Raven, exultant,
Gave a joyous note
To the Great Lady mother.

The Partridge then she sang,
I'm going to build my nest
Inside that stable.
So, I may see the Child
And watch when he trembles
In his mothers arms.

In Mexico 'P' is for Christmas

The following account is edited from accounts kindly given by His Excellency, the Mexican Ambassador, in 1984.

Piñatas, *Presepio, Posadas* and poinsettias are the chief ingredients of a Mexican Christmas, which is a colourful fiesta combining Meso-american and Spanish cultures.

The first is the *Posada* which means 'the inn'. It originated in Colonial times when the Franciscan Fathers, wishing to make the story of the Birth of Christ more attractive and accessible, had the idea of a *novena* festival between 16 and 24 December. Nine in honour of the nine months that Mary was expecting. In addition, these nine days commemorate the pilgrimage of Joseph and Mary from the time they left their humble home in Nazareth to fulfil Caesar's edict to make a census, and their arrival in Bethlehem. The holy couple thus become pilgrims, begging for lodging in the little villages they passed on the way.

The tradition of the *Posadas* tells us in simple verses how the couple arrive at Bethlehem, and find no room at the inn. The procession of Mary, on a donkey led by an angel, and Joseph go from village to village or house to house asking for lodging:

> 'In the name of Heaven,
> I beg you for lodging
> So that here may rest
> My beloved wife'

Each time they are turned down:

> 'This is no Inn
> Be on your way
> I will not open
> For you may be some rogue'

The verses continue in pleading and refusal until at last one opens, and the joyous celebration begins as Mary bestows gifts on her benefactors, cinnamon fudge, candies, almonds and peanuts. The happy end to the *Posada* was, and still is, the *Piñata*. Full of seasonal fruit, it was traditionally in the form of a star to recall the one which guided the Kings to the Baby Jesus. In the olden days the last *Posada* on Christmas Eve was the best because it was followed by Midnight Mass, and the whole village would follow the procession to the church.

Possibly the element which the children look forward to most of all is the *Piñata*. Made from clay, and painted brightly, it is filled with fruits, sweets and toys, and hung from a tree. The children, blindfold, hit out at it with sticks until it finally breaks and they are all showered with the gifts. The shape varies: it can be a traditional star or a lantern shape, a bull or another animal or many others – the similarity is in the colouring – it is as bright as bright can be, with reds and blues and yellows and greens and bright pinks. And it is then decorated with ribbons and paper streamers.

Since the Second World War, it has been more common for each small neighbourhood group to hold its own *Posada* and *Piñata*, usually in one house, where there is a set procession of prayers and visits to each room to find the *Presepio*, the manger. On the last evening, in a room at the very top of the house, it is found.

The *Pastorales* are Nativity plays similar to the medieval mystery plays of Europe and they have their origins in these too, having been introduced by the missionaries. They are a mixture of the sacred and comedy as the 'evil' one is thwarted.

The last 'P' is for poinsettias. The name of this flower is the Christmas Eve Flower, because it blooms then. The historian, Aragón Leyva, speaks of its origins thus: 'they called it *Cuetlaóchiti*, which means, "the flower that fades", and the Franciscan friars carried this flower to the altar and thus bedecked the Feast of Christmas, a custom that was traditional in the South in what today are the states of Morelos and Guerrero'. It is said

Children in Mexico look forward to the old tradition of breaking the Piñata, painted by Dorothy Barron. The Society of Nativitists, 1985.

that this tradition goes back four hundred years. The spread of this flower to other parts of the world is thanks to the American diplomat, Joel Poinsett, who took it to his country and gave it its name.

Such an old flower has to have its legend and here is the legend of the poinsettia:

> On a Christmas Eve long ago, a poor boy was crying at the door of his little church, because he was so very poor that he had no gift to bring to the manger. He dared not enter the church without a gift, so knelt outside to say his prayers, 'I do so want to bring a gift for the Holy Baby, but I am very poor and dread to approach you with empty hands,' he prayed. When he finally arose, he turned to walk away and saw there at his feet flowers springing up from the earth with leaves of the brightest red. He gathered some of the lovely plants and joyously entered the church with his gift for the baby Jesus.

And that is why the plant has become the symbol of Christmas giving in Mexico.

How to Say 'Merry Christmas' in Brazil

The following account of Christmas traditions in Brazil is from a newspaper article sent to the author by the Brazilian Embassy. The article is about twenty years old and some of the customs have died away since, but it shows a nostalgic side of Christmas as it used to be in sunny Brazil.

Christmas in Brazil was originally observed by the keeping of customs brought to the New World by the Portuguese. Later, many were modified by Indian and African influences. In recent years both European and American traditions have replaced to a great extent the old-style Christmas in many parts of the country.

Although Christmas falls in the heart of the Brazilian summer, Santa Claus – 'Papai-Noel', as he is called here – arrives bedecked in his red flannel suit, rubber boots and famous whiskers glistening with artificial snow.

Brazilian Christmas is a time for family reunions, games, music, dancing and banquets. Nativity scenes appear throughout the land. In Rio, São Paulo and other urban areas, 'Natal' is nowadays celebrated with great splendour and munificence in contrast with former times when Christmas festivities were limited to attending church, and gifts for the family.

Although there are various regional interpretations as to the way of observing Christ's birth in Brazil, there is universal accord on the erection of the 'Presepio', the Nativity, and celebration of Midnight Mass.

After Mass everyone goes home to a Christmas supper. The traditional dish is Roast Turkey with 'Farafa' (raisins, nuts and dried fruits). Roast suckling pig is served by many families, and in the North there is seafood.

The most authentic Christmas in the historic sense, however, is the celebration which takes place in rural areas, where outside influences have taken longer to penetrate. In these regions the Indo-Luso-Afro influence holds full sway. To a country already rich in folklore these rural and somewhat primitive Christmas observances, by their simplicity, add much that is beautiful and picturesque.

In the rural areas of North-eastern Brazil they have a custom called the *BumbaMeu-Boi*. This folk tradition has been observed for more than 120 years. It is a combination of a dance, a game and a satirical play, which all the townsfolk participate in, with the *Burrinho* as a central figure. *Burrinho* is a hobbyhorse-type donkey with a man to 'ride' it.

Other features preserved are the *Reisado*, Festival of the Three Kings, in which groups of costumed players wearing crowns, festooned with ribbons and carrying tambourines, go around seeking alms for the poor. The songs they sing may be humorous or in praise of the life of Christ. Then there is *Pastorinha*, a religious folk play based on the nativity scene in Bethlehem. The play is climaxed by the dismantling of the coconut fronds forming the crèche, which are then carried away by a group of maidens, and burnt. The celebration of *Folia dos Roi* (Frolics of the Kings) consists mainly of a dance. Dancers are accompanied from village to village by drummers, guitarists, and tambourine players. The troubadours, who start out on Christmas Eve, end their march on 2 February, the Day of Our Lady of the Candles, with a big supper.

Junkanoo

A FESTIVAL IN THE BAHAMAS

In the Bahamas there is a most unusual and legendary festival at Christmas called Junkanoo. There are several claims concerning origin, but most people accept that it relates to a benefactor by the name of John Canoe. Whatever its origins it has continued, despite several attempts to ban it, from the early part of the nineteenth century to this day. The following account is from the Ministry of Culture, together with some contemporary newspaper reports. It gives a valuable insight into the controversy surrounding the origin of the oldest West Indian festival, John Canoe. The festival is believed to be a quaint survival of an old African slave custom practised by the slaves who came to the Americas in the sixteenth and seventeenth centuries.

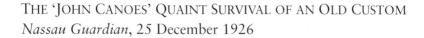

THE 'JOHN CANOES' QUAINT SURVIVAL OF AN OLD CUSTOM
Nassau Guardian, 25 December 1926

Every Christmastide someone asks the origin of the 'Johnny Canoe' custom which is one of the oldest of West Indian customs and was observed in the old days we believe, in some of the Southern States although it has survived longer in the Bahamas than elsewhere. It has been difficult to trace the origin and one of our readers has discovered the following in an old West Indian review for 1817 which throws interesting light on the subject:

> Johnny Canoe. A festivity in honourable memorial of John Conny, a celebrated cabaeero at Tres Puntas in Ascim, on the Guiney Coast, who flourished around 1720. He bore great authority among the Negroes of that district. When the Prussians deserted Fort Brandenburg they left it to his charge and he gallantly held it for a long time against the Dutch to whom it was afterwards ceded by the Prussian monarch.

In the Nassau Guardian's *account of Christmas Day 1898, Bay Street in particular came alive at a very early hour with scores of masked men who created amusement for the spectators. Two prominent features of nineteenth-century John Canoe were masks and fringed garments. Masqueraders usually powdered or painted their faces and wore home-made headdresses. In time headgear and masks developed. Masks were usually formed from a wire base and papier mâché applied. At times, brown paper bags and/or crocus sacks were used to make John Canoe masks.*
In A winter in Paradise *by Allan Parsons (1924), there is a very vivid description of John Canoe.*

Christmas Eve, 1924
In the evening out into Bay Street to see the beginning of the Christmas orgies of the natives. This is a very strange and primitive business. From 8 to 12 p.m. and again from 4 till 8.30 a.m., arrayed in the most fantastic fancy costumes, all the natives march up and down Bay Street beating tom-toms and blowing trumpets. It is a queer survival of their African origins. The noise is terrific. They are apparently moderately sober, and don't fight much;

quite respectful to the spectators, and only intent, as one so often used to be at Oxford, on getting as much noise as possible out of one's own musical instrument.

Christmas Day, 1924
Sleep was obviously impossible tonight during this island festival. The lady of the house obviously thought the same, for at 5.30 a.m. she began to discourse the 'March of the Toy Soldiers' on the pianola with such runs and roulades as would have made Artur Rubinstein envious.

Dancing man at the Junkanoo parade. Nassau Magazine, *1935.*

Viola got up at 6 and I at 6.30 to go down to the quarters of the Nassauvians' Club in Bay Street to witness the remainder of the orgies. There, only just awake, I was received by a most courteous member, who offered me champagne. This I felt I could not face, but had a cup of strong coffee.

The orgies lasted till 8.30, at which hour all the participants melted into thin air in the most orderly manner. The process was the same, just marching up and down with the tom-toms, but some of the costumes were most imaginative. They all had white masks or had whitened their faces.

One was dressed like the Englishman in the Boutique, another had a Shakespearean costume of red velvet with a trench hat; there were three Highlanders, and a quantity decked out as women in the latest Paris fashions.

One man especially pleased me: his face grotesquely whitened, on his head was a little clown's cap, for the rest he was dressed entirely in flour bags. Over his shoulder he carried a vast bundle of sugarcanes, and his middle was wreathed around with twenty or thirty bananas. On the end of a knotted string he held a Whippet. . . .

The Changing Face of Japan

Edited from various accounts

The Japanese were introduced to Christmas as long ago as the seventeenth century by missionaries sent to convert them to Christianity. Since then there has been an erratic relationship with Christianity and its customs: pockets of Japan became Christianized, other areas remained Shinto or Buddhist. However, Christmas became a part of their industry in the early twentieth century. As British allies they manufactured lights and cake decorations, slipping neatly into the slot left by the Germans after the First World War and their export trade continuing after the Second World War under American occupation.

With the American influence and homesick American GIs desperately attempting to create Christmas away from home, the Japanese living in areas of occupation often adopted some of their customs. One account tells of a small girl who remembers her father leaving a decorated Christmas tree on the doorstep for his daughters to find. She remembers being almost afraid of the ugly beaded decorations on it!

The Japanese love to give presents and so the customs of giftgiving associated with Christmas caught on well. Now in most cities the department stores have huge decorated and illuminated Christmas trees, and some even have Christmas displays and Christmas shops. Hankyu in Osaka and Tokyo held a huge Victorian Christmas exhibition one year covering a whole floor of their store. While Felissimo, who have their main offices in Kobe, have a Christmas shop, beautifully illuminated by Italian lighting display specialists, and a museum and shop of Christmas in Hakodate. In Tokyo there is a German Christmas market.

Children in the kindergartens have decorated playrooms and are sometimes given small presents. Mostly the emphasis is on the commercial side of Christmas and Christianity exists only in a few very small areas. The following short account from just before the First World War by a teacher, Miss Wynne Willson, shows a different side.

'Only three months till Christmas' said Fujiko san, as she sat on the swing one bright October day, with Oharu san, a new arrival at the school. 'What is Christmas?' asked Oharu san, 'Is it a "matsuri" (idol festival) of the foreign teachers?' 'Yes, it is the "iwai" (rejoicing) at the birth of Jesus the Saviour, but it is a joy for all the world, not only for the "gaijin" (foreigners). All have on their most beautiful clothes, and strings of red lanterns are hung in the playground, and many guests are invited, and the big schoolroom is decorated with flags, and the great curtain with the school crest is hung round the walls, and in the middle is some wonderful thing, perhaps a

Japanese children in a celebration parade, c. 1900.

tree full of lights; last year it was a well, just like a real one.

First we sing carols – that is, songs about Christmas – then a strange "ojisan" (old gentleman) comes in a long white beard and his dress all white with wool, which is meant for the snow that comes in the twelfth month in foreign countries. They call him "Father Christmas". He says many amusing things, and invites us to come and look at the splendid thing in the middle of the room, and then each one receives a present from it. Last year out of that well, we each drew a lovely foreign doll. Mine had golden hair and a pink dress and eyes that open and shut. I took it home in the summer and my mother could not let go of it in case it might break. But she kept it in a drawer alone, and when she feels lonely, she takes it out and admires it. Then after presents we sing again, and each receives a beautiful box of cakes.'

A small round-eyed girl was listening eagerly to Fujiko's talk. Now she chimed in eagerly, 'Ah! Christmas is delightful, better than New Year, better than the Doll's Festival.'

Christmas in the school was celebrated on the 23rd, because many of the girls went home for Christmas as most were from Christian families. Fujiko went home to her widowed mother who had her home in the rice fields.

There at the little Christian church, some people were busy making wreaths to hang above the sliding paper doors. At nine o'clock on Christmas morning the little church was nearly full. Rows of people sitting on their heels, their shoes left in neat rows at the back. It was a special time also for the new Christians who were to be baptised into 'the Religion' on that special day.

After the service the teachers called for silence, and some big doors were slid open, and disclosed a tall glittering Christmas tree, from which all kinds of fruit were picked in the shape of small toys, costing only about half a penny each, but treasures to the children. Then came bright papers full of crisp biscuits called 'Sembei', and five golden oranges apiece called 'Satsumas'. All were received with a demure little bow, and then the little bare feet were slipped into their 'Geta' and they scampered away into the bright sunshine.

But Christmas was not over yet. There were speeches, and then refreshments in the shape of straw-coloured tea in tiny bowls, and gorgeous green and pink cakes (made from rice or sugar) which looked nicer than they tasted – so the English Missionary thought. Then followed games of all kinds, and much talking and laughter before it was time to go home.

Mirror Image Customs

Hirokatsu Onishi; translated by Akio Onishi

These old customs whose origins are lost in time have distinct similarities to many Western customs – the Namahage is like the Hairy Hordes from Central European regions and its visit is similar to the visit to Wales of the Mari Lwyd; the Welsh also decorated a holly tree in some areas. The custom of throwing out beans to release the demons is similar to the European custom of taking down all the Christmas decorations in the house by twelfth night or bad luck will befall the occupants. The most interesting feature of this is the fact that originally the date for taking down evergreens was 2 February, thereby releasing the wood spirits which had sheltered in the house during the winter. Mr Hirokatsu Onishi, government official of the prefecture of Gifu, reports the following:

Santa Claus turned up in Japan in 1875, and the first book of Christmas was published in 1898 called, *Santakuro* and was a book about Santa Claus and for children.

The following account is not directly related to Christmas, but has a similarity to such European Christmas characters as *Crampus* and *Knecht Ruprecht*. [These are scary characters from Alpine tradition throughout Europe, which nowadays are part of the Santa Claus entourage.]

Namahage has appeared in the snowy villages every 15th [January]. He visits the houses in the village wearing the mask of a demon and clothes made of straw and carries a box which he rattles and it makes a scary noise. When he visits the houses he says, 'Where are your naughty children?' The children are afraid of him. The people living in the houses have to give him food and drink and entertain him, and then say, 'My children are nice' to make him go away.

Also, *Shi-Shi-Mai* and *Shichi Fukugin* come to the houses on New Year's Day. This custom is like old Father Christmas in Britain when people

Modern Japanese Christmas foods, including the buttercream Christmas cake. Courtesy of Mariko Akama.

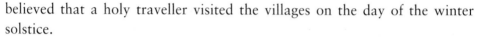

believed that a holy traveller visited the villages on the day of the winter solstice.

We have another custom like the Christmas tree custom. People decorate a pine tree in front of their houses on New Year's Day, and long ago some areas had the custom of cutting the pine tree, which had to be done on 13 December.

We also decorate a holly tree, and put the head of an eagle on the door on the day of the beginning of spring which is traditionally 3 February. On this day we throw beans to let the demons out.

PREPARATIONS AND VICTUALS

Standing Pie

English pork pies are steeped in history. They are part of the heritage of the Viking past and the last vestige of the great Christmas pies. Now the most famous are the Melton Mowbray pies, but in fact at Christmas time pork butchers all over England will make a pile of these delectable savoury pies for the Christmas buffet, to be served with pickles and chutneys. The following recipe is from Yorkshire where Christmas pies originated many hundreds of years ago. Originally made from hot-water pastry, which is both cholesterol-laden and indigestible, the following recipe uses short pastry and should be baked in a spring-sided cake tin. These quantities will fill one 10-inch tin.

Filling ingredients:
1 lb lean diced pork
1 lb unsmoked bacon bits
1 medium sharp baking apple, grated
1 large onion, peeled and grated

1 teaspoon freshly grated root ginger (if liked)
1 teaspoon any other spice you like (garlic, nutmeg, paprika)
about six leaves fresh rubbed sage (or dried if fresh not available)
pepper to taste; no salt, the bacon provides enough

Short pastry ingredients:
1 lb plain flour
1 lb sunflower fat such as Trex
pinch of salt and water to mix

Method:
Rough line a cake tin with a large single piece of baking parchment, big enough to cover bottom and sides. This is important or you will not be able to unmould the baked pie.

Roll out a circle of pastry large enough to cover bottom and sides in one piece. Lift it into the tin on a rolling pin. If you have a break or a gap, don't worry. It can be filled with extra bits of pastry.

Mix all your meats and spices together with the grated apple and onion and press into the pastrycase right to the top, slightly rounded off.

Preheat your oven to 180°C/220°C conventional elec./425°F/Gas 7. Cover with another round of pastry, moisten the sides and press the lid to the sides to seal. Make a hole in the centre, brush with milk and bake for 10 minutes on high, then turn oven down to 160°C/180°C/350°F/Gas 4–5 and bake for about 2 hours. Cover the top of the pie with foil if it begins to get too dark, or turn your oven down a bit more.

While it is baking, boil two pig's trotters (from the butcher) in a pan of water seasoned with salt, pepper, nutmeg and bay. This will produce a delicious jellied stock. When the pie is completely cold, and before you unmould it, pour some of the warmed stock through the hole. This will set into a jelly around the meat. Leave pie well covered in the fridge for two days before unmoulding. It can be frozen for up to three months. Wrap loosely in foil and freeze in the tin. Unmould when well frozen.

Serve in slices with pickled onion, chutneys, etc.

Great Grandmother's Christmas in Dublin

The following account is a melting pot of accounts and reminiscences from a number of relatives and acquaintances whose roots are firmly set in Irish soil, mostly around County Cork and Dublin, and accompanied by records from the Dublin Historical Archives.

The market was a very fine thing to be sure. Especially the Christmas Eve market, that was special. Everyone hung around enjoying the atmosphere, gossiping with old friends, until the end of the day, when the twilight was low, then they would buy. By then the stallholders had put down the prices, almost throwing some things at you they were, which would not keep over Christmas. 'Will ye be putting that big chicken down yet?' asks a shopper, for perhaps the third time. But the shrewd stallholder is hanging on till the bitter end in the hopes of selling at a better price.

In the 1880s, when I was a girl, the Christmas markets began about three or four days beforehand. We would go down with our father after work to look at the displays of toys.

A Dublin newspaper from 1920 had the following account written by someone remembering Christmas some forty-odd years previously:

About three days before Christmas the country carts arrived, laden down with slaughtered fowl, taking up their positions along the south side of the street. A long line extending from James's Street up to and often into High Street, fifty to a hundred of them. The horses were unhitched and taken to the stables and yards. The shafts lowered, and an old countrywoman would take her seat on this elevation, with all the skewered fowl laid out on the straw. From there she dictated the terms of purchase. There was continuous haggling and a good deal of good humour and teasing, as well as blessing and cursing. For the time being the cart is her home; here she sleeps under a large, faded umbrella, she has brought her breakfast, dinner

The Wren Boys bringing good luck and begging a penny and a bit o' cake in Ireland, c. 1880s.

and tea, making herself comfortable with a couple of heavy shawls and many petticoats, and from her seat she will not move except on the stress of necessity. In some cases, the old farmer would mount guard while his wife and daughter ran across the street to Jacob's Restaurant for their meals.

When the weather was fine and business good, the life was pleasant enough, and the old country folk enjoyed the experience. But on frosty and bitter nights the sellers were nearly frozen to their seats. A heavy snowstorm would bury seller and birds under its white mantle, worse was the rain, with a pitiless cold soaking into the skin.

Though sales might be slack in the daytime, the night-time made amends. There was a great throng in Thomas Street during the days of the fair, with any amount of sport, jostling and shouting, horseplay and unfortunately a good deal of drinking. The shops were all brilliantly lit up and kept open to a late hour. The many booths in the street were illuminated with kerosene lamps and blazing ducklamps. There were great displays of cheap toys and cards and presents, cooking utensils and certain kinds of food. Huge heaps of holly and ivy were piled in the streets and mistletoe was not wanting either. Boys made a nuisance blowing bugles and horns and swinging rattles noisily.

The Christmas Eve market was especially interesting. A large number of buyers postponing their purchase till the last minute in the hope of getting the big bargain.

It was the custom in rural Ireland for the menfolk to tidy the farmyards and paint all the farm buildings with fresh limewash. Then they would paint the house inside and out the same. The women would sweep and clean and polish till everything shone. Only then would they get on with the baking. Anything up to four generations of womenfolk around the big scrubbed table kneading bread, mixing the cakes and rolling out the pastry. Everyone who could would go to the midnight mass, going in the horse-drawn buggies if the church was some distance carrying torches of bog-fir. It was a wonderful sight to see all the flickering lights of the torches, as people came on foot, by trap or on horseback from all directions to the church. Bog-fir is a woody root especially split and dried and bound around for the Christmas Eve trip to Church. It burns long and bright. Afterwards back home to sit around the banked up peat fire and sup a hot drink before falling into bed for a few short hours. There was another mass at dawn, and for those near enough, yet another mid-morning. Christmas Day was the only day that the priest could say three masses.

The animals had to be tended, Christmas Day or no. This was done with a good will, with extra feed all round. The mucking out done quickly into a corner of the yard until the next day.

Christmas afternoon everyone visited everyone else. The big fruit cake was cut again and again, and the hot tea and the whisky handed round, while someone always had an old fiddle to play, and those energetic enough would dance. Christmas was short and simple, but people enjoyed it in all its simplicity. They prepared with great energy for the big day, they gave thanks and praise where it was due, and they enjoyed their rest. What more did we want?

Our Arbre de Noël

From A Versailles Christmastide by Mary Stuart Boyd

This tale is set at the end of 1900, and tells the story of English parents who travel to France to collect their son, referred to as 'the Boy', from school for the Christmas holidays. They discover he and a classmate have contracted scarlet fever and he is not fit to travel. There is nothing to be done but to rent rooms and spend Christmas in Versailles. The story is written in an autobiographical style, by Mrs Boyd, who was well known for her travelogues. The story creates an accurate picture of the typical Christmas experienced by an expatriate in France in the late years of the nineteenth century. The motorcar is beginning to infiltrate Versailles from Paris and the soldiers are on alert expecting war with Germany, while in England the Boer War is well under way. In Versailles the Christmas tree is only heard of and is rarely used, being a 'toy' for the wealthy, and there were only a few wealthy, people after the fall of the Second Empire. The crib is the main focus of Christmas.

We bought it on the Sunday morning from old Grand-mère Gomard in the Avenue de St Cloud.

It was not a noble specimen of a tree. Looked at with cold, unimaginative eyes, it might have been considered lop-sided; undersized it undoubtedly was. Yet a pathetic familiarity in the desolate aspect of the little tree aroused our sympathy as no rare horticultural trophy ever could.

Some Christmas fairy must have whispered to Grand-mère to grub up the tiny tree and to include it in the stock she was taking to Versailles on the market morning. For there it was, its roots stuck securely into a big pot, looking like some forlorn forest bantling among the garden plants.

Grand-mère Gomard had established herself in a cosy nook at the foot of one of the great leafless trees of the Avenue. Straw hurdles were cunningly arranged to form three sides of a square, in whose midst she was seated on a rushbottomed chair, like a queen on a humble throne. Her head was bound by a gaily striped kerchief, and her feet rested snugly on a charcoal stove.

'Grand-mère' in her cosy nook, from A Versailles Christmastide, 1902.

Her merchandise, which consisted of half a dozen pots of pink and white primulas, a few spotted or crimson cyclamen, sundry lettuce and cauliflower plants, and some roots of pansies and daisies, was grouped around her.

The primulas and cyclamen, though their pots were shrouded in pinafores of white paper skilfully calculated to conceal any undue lankiness of stem, left us unmoved. But the sight of the starveling little fir tree reminded us that at the hospital lay two sick boys whose roseate dreams of London and holidays had suddenly changed to the knowledge that weeks of isolation and imprisonment behind the window-blinds with the red cross lay before them. If we could not give them the longed-for home Christmas, we could at least give them a Christmas tree.

The sight of foreign customers for Grand-mère Gomard speedily collected a small group of interested spectators. A knot of children relinquishing their tantalizing occupation of hanging round the pan of charcoal, over whose glow chestnuts were cracking appetizingly, and the stall of the lady who with amazing celerity fried pancakes (*crêpes*) on a hot plate, and sold them dotted with butter and sprinkled with sugar to the lucky possessors of a sou. Even the sharp urchin who presided over the old umbrella, which, reversed, with the ferrule fixed in a cross-bar of wood, served as a receptacle for sheets of festive note-paper, embellished with lace edges and further adorned with coloured scraps, temporarily entrusting a juvenile sister with his responsibilities, added his presence to our court.

Christmas trees seemed not to be greatly in demand in Versailles, and many were the whispered communings as to what '*Les Anglais*' proposed doing with the tree after they had bought it. When the transaction was completed and Grand-mère Gomard had exchanged the tree, with a sheet of *La Patrie* wrapped around its pot, for a franc and our thanks, the interest increased. We would require someone to carry our purchase, and each of the bright eyed, short cropped Jeans and Pierres was eager to offer himself. But our selection was already made. A slender boy in beret and black pinafore, who had been our earliest spectator, was singled out and entrusted with our '*arbre de Noël*' to our hotel.

The fact that it had met with approbation appeared to encourage the little tree. The change may have been imaginary, but from the moment it passed into our possession the branches seemed less despondent, the needles more erect.

'Will you put toys on it?' the youthful porter asked suddenly.

'Yes; it is for a sick boy – a boy who has a fever. Have you ever had an *arbre de Noël*?'

'*Jamais*', was his conclusive reply: the tone thereof suggesting that was a felicity quite beyond the range of possibility.

The tree secured, there began the comparatively difficult work of finding the customary ornaments of glass and glitter to deck it. A fruitless search had left us almost in despair, when, late on Monday afternoon, we joyed to discover miniature candles of red, yellow, and blue on the open air stall in front of a toy-store. A rummage in the interior of the shop procured candle clips, and a variety of glittering bagatelles. Laden with treasure, we hurried back to the hotel, and began the work of decoration in preparation for the morning.

Selecting a Christmas present, from A Versailles Christmastide, *1902.*

During its short stay in our room at the hotel, the erstwhile despised little tree met with an adulation that must have warmed the heart within the rough stem. When nothing more than the three coloured glass globes, a gilded walnut, and a gorgeous humming bird with wings and tail of spun glass had been suspended by narrow ribbon from its branches, Rosine, the pretty Swiss chambermaid, chancing to enter the room with letters, was struck with admiration and pronounced it '*très belle!*'

And Karl bringing in a fresh panier of logs when the adorning was complete, and the silly little delightful sparkle twinkled from every spray, putting down his burden, threw up his hands in amazement and declared the *arbre de Noël* '*Magnifique!*'

This alien Christmas tree had an element all its own. When we were searching for knick-knacks the shops were full of tiny Holy Babes lying cradled in waxen innocence in mangers of yellow corn. One of these little effigies we bought because they pleased us. And when the decoration of the tree was nearly complete the tip of the central stem standing scraggily naked called for covering, what more fitting than that the dear little Sacred Babe in his nest of golden straw should have the place of honour?

It was late on Christmas Eve before our task was ended. But next morning when Karl, carrying in our *petit déjeûner*, turned on the electric light, and our anxious gaze sought our work, we found it good.

Then followed a hurried packing of the loose presents; and, a *fiacre* having been summoned, the tree which had entered the room in all humility passed out transmogrified beyond knowledge. Rosine, duster in hand, leant over the bannister of the upper landing to watch its descent. Karl saw it coming and flew to open the outer door for its better egress. Even the stout old driver of the red-wheeled cab creaked cumbrously round on his box to look upon its beauties.

The Market was busy in the square as we rattled through. From behind their battlemented wares the country mice waged war with the town mice over the price of the merchandise. But on this occasion we were too engrossed to notice a scene whose picturesque humour usually fascinated us, for as the carriage jogged over the rough roads the poor little *arbre de Noël* palpitated convulsively. The gee-gaws clattered like castanets, as though in frantic expostulation, and the radiant spun glass humming-birds quivered until we expected them to break from their elastic fetters and fly away. The scarlet and green one with the gold flecked wings fell to the floor and rolled under the seat just as the cab drew up at the great door of the school.

From her window, the concièrge of the Red Cross hospital nodded her approval, and at the door of the hospital the good *Soeur* received us, a flush of pleasure glorifiying her tranquil face.

Then followed a moment wherein the patients were ordered to shut their eyes, to reopen them upon the splendid vision of the *arbre de Noël*. Perhaps its was the contrast of the meagre background of the tiny school hospital, with its two white beds and bare walls, but, placed in full view on the central table, the tree was almost imposing. It was just the right size for the surroundings.

A donor who is handicapped by the knowledge that the gifts he selects must within a few weeks be destroyed by fire,* is rarely lavish in his outlay. Yet our presents, wrapped in white paper and tied with blue ribbons, when arranged round the flowerpot, made a wonderful display. There were mounted Boers, who when you pressed the ball at the end of the air-tube, galloped in a wobbly fashion. The invalids had good fun later trying to race them, and 'the Boy' professed to find that his Boer gained an accelerated speed when he whispered 'Bobs' to him. There were tales of adventure, flasks of cologne, and smart virile pocket-books, one red morocco, one blue.

---

* All contagious illnesses meant that the personal property of patients would be burnt afterwards.

We regretted the pocket books, but their possession made the recipients, who, boylike, took no heed for the cleansing fires of tomorrow, feel grown up at once. For the sister there was a tiny gold consecrated medal. A small tribute for our esteem, but one that pleased the devout recipient.

Suspended among the purely ornamental trinkets of the tree hung tiny net bags of crystallized violets, and many large chocolates rolled up in silver paper. The boys, who had subsisted for days on nothing more exciting than boiled milk, openly rejoiced when they caught sight of the sweets. But to her patients' disgust, the *Soeur*, who had a pretty wit of her own, promptly frustrated their intentions by counting the dainties.

'I count the chocolates. They are good boys, wise boys, honest boys, and I have every confidence in them – but, I count the chocolates!', she said.

As we passed back along the Rue de la Paroisse, worshippers were flocking in and out of Notre Dame, running the gauntlet of the unsavoury beggars who, loudly importunate, thronged the portals. Before the quiet nook wherein, under a gold be-starred canopy, was the tableau of the Infant Jesus in the stable, little children stood in wide-eyed adoration, and older people gazed with mute adoration.

Some might deem the little spectacle theatrical, and there was a slight irrelevance in the pot plants that were grouped along the foreground, but none could fail to be impressed by the silent reverence of the congregation. No service was in progress, yet many believers knelt in prayer. Here a pretty girl gave thanks for evident blessings received; there an old spinster, the narrowness of whose means forbade her expending a couple of sous on the hire of a chair, knelt on the chilly flags and murmured words of gratitude for benefits whereof her appearance bore no outward indication.

We had left the 'prisoners' to the enjoyment of their newly acquired property in the morning. At gloaming we again mounted the time-worn outside stair leading to the chamber whose casement bore the ominous red cross. The warm glow of firelight filled the room, scintillating in the glittering facets of the baubles on the tree; and from their pillows two pale-faced boys – boys who, despite their lengthening limbs were yet happy children at heart, watched eager-eyed while the sweet-faced *Soeur*, with reverential care, lit the candles that surrounded the Holy Babe.

Liver for Christmas in Greece?

The two major religious feasts in Greece are of course Easter and Christmas, and these are marked all over Greece by customs that are universal in character but differ in detail from place to place. Compared with New Year's Day, Christmas is less important in Greece than in most other Christian countries, but it has nevertheless become an occasion for gifts, parties and decorated fir trees. In Greece the traditional red-robed Santa Claus appears in the guise of St Basil and, on both Christmas Eve and New Year's Eve, children go from house to house singing carols and collecting drachmas.

Especially in the countryside, the chief preparations for Christmas centre around the Christmas table. After a long period of fasting, the time has come to slaughter the turkey or the pig which the family have been fattening since mid-summer. On Christmas Eve too every housewife without fail bakes a *Christopsomo*, literally 'Christbread'. This is made in large sweet loaves of various shapes, with decorated images carved on the crust, usually representing some aspect of the family's life and work. Thus in Macedonia, a farmer's Christmas loaf will often be decorated with lambs, kids and a sheepfold. Also it is unthinkable to forget the poor on Christmas Day. At Koroni in Messinia, for example, the first slice from the Christmas loaf is given to the first beggar who happens to pass the house. Another common custom is to pour a few drops of oil or wine on the hearth. This is a survival from libations of the ancient Greeks to the Goddess Hestia whose symbol was the hearth.

On such an occasion when the whole family is gathered round the Christmas table, it is natural that the dead should be remembered as well. Hence at Christmas time visits to the cemetery and offerings to the dead are still made. The cult of the dead, though, takes many different forms. On the island of Nisyros, for example, in the Dodecanese, the priest holds a brief service on Christmas evening after which he distributes the victuals for this purpose to the faithful. At Lassithi in Crete the housewife fries some liver on Christmas Day and takes it to the church, together with a bottle of wine and a bun, to be blessed and distributed after the liturgy.

On New Year's Eve family reunions and parties share the custom of cutting the *vasilopita*, or Basil Cake, for good luck in the coming year. Like the Western Christmas pudding, the 'vasilopita' contains a coin, usually a gold sovereign, which is reckoned to bring luck for the rest of the year to whoever finds it in his piece of cake. This custom is observed in the cities and larger towns as well, although there the *vasilopita* is not always baked at home, but may well be bought at a confectioner's; while in the villages it is made with more spices and is more elaborately decorated. It is cut by the master of the house first cutting a slice for St Basil, then a slice for the house, and then one for each member of the household. There may also be one for the cattle and one for the poor. In the Pontus and in Cappadocia the coin used to be stuck into an orange or an apple, following the tradition in Byzantium, but this custom varies from place to place.

This is Christmas American Style!

In America there are several villages which are Santa 'hideaways', when he is visiting the far side of the world. There's the Christmas village in Torrington, Connecticut, which was erected every Christmas. Santa's Workshop is said to exist on Whiteface Mountain, Wilmington, which is situated near Lake Placid in New York. It was built in 1949 by Arto Monaco, who had previously worked for Walt Disney.
But the original is a town actually named after the fine old gent – Santa Claus, Indiana. The story began in 1882, and it is a town which is a 'theme park'. Imagine living in a theme park! Christmas every day and if you tire of the usual Sunday roast you can always go out to lunch at one of the town's seasonal restaurants. The Christmas Room, where they serve turkey with all the Christmas trimmings, or the Three Kings Food Fair for a quick hot-dog, before popping into Mrs Klaus's kitchen for some home-made cookies to take home for tea! This is Christmas America. The following extract is from the press release for the town:

Santa Claus, Indiana

For more than 130 years now it's been Christmas every day in this small Southern Indiana hamlet, which for the past 50 odd years has attracted hundreds of thousands of visitors to visit its namesake Theme Park, Santa Claus Land.

Long before there was a Disneyworld, there was a Santa Claus Land. In fact Santa Claus Land in Santa Claus, Indiana was the original of all such theme parks as they exist today.

Appropriately it was a child who provided the inspiration in naming this community after Santa Claus. Going into the late fall [autumn] months of 1852, there was no Santa Claus Community. Residents of the area spent months trying to select a name for the community, but none of those suggested carried universal appeal.

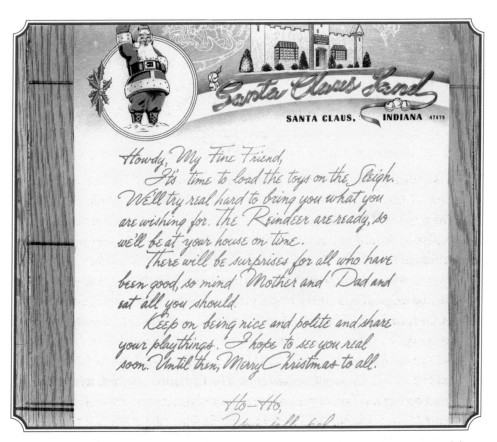

A copy of a letter sent by Santa Claus, from Santa Claus, Indiana, 1940s. Courtesy of the Santa Claus Village.

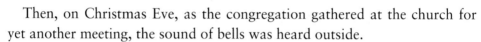

Then, on Christmas Eve, as the congregation gathered at the church for yet another meeting, the sound of bells was heard outside.

'Santa', a jubilant child rang out. 'It's Santa Claus'.

'That's it!' shouted one of the elders. 'Why not call it Santa Claus!'

The residents all agreed, and the town of Santa Claus was born. Except for the addition of the US Post Office in 1856, the town remained a quaint community tucked away in the rolling hills of Southern Indiana. It would take until 1933 before the community started to match its unique name to some equally unique attractions. . . .

Originally opened as Santa Claus Land in 1946, making it the oldest theme park in the United States, it has grown constantly. In 1965 the population was only 64. By 1986 there were nearer 750 residents in an area of 2,000 acres, making it the largest town area in the whole of Spenser County.

Santa's Village, California, is a purpose-built theme park. Tucked away amidst pine trees it was built in 1955 and here you can sample Christmas all the year round, enjoy a hay-ride and eat things like cornbread or marsh-mallows on toast. And, of course, meet Santa.

Christmas Towns

The USA can boast a number of towns and places named after Christmas including: Christmas Lake – Scott County, Minnesota; Christmas – Bolivar County, Mississippi; Christmas – Lawrence County, Kentucky; Christmas – Roane County, Tennessee; Christmas – Gila County, Arizona; Christmas – Orange County, Florida.

Christmas in July

Many Americans cannot wait until Christmas for their celebrations and have 'Christmas in July', Mrs Klara Johnson writes of her Christmas in July dinner, complete with turkey, a Christmas tree and guests bringing little gifts to exchange.

Thousands more Americans join together in clubs which collect Christmas memorabilia: whether it is solid silver tree ornaments, angels, antique decorations, the Americans have a club for it. The biggest is 'The Golden Glow of Christmas Past', founded some twenty years ago by Jerry Ehernberger. Members have a glorious Christmas get-together which is a cross between an antique market, a congress and a Christmas party.

The Ultimate Christmas Store

For the ultimate in Christmas shopping experience there is Bronner's Christmas Wonderland, whose address is, appropriately, 25 Christmas Lane. Its founder, Wally Bronner, founded the store in his home town of Frankenmuth, Michigan. A devout Lutheran, Wally believed that you could blend good business with Christian charity and religious feeling. His store's motto is: "Enjoy CHRISTmas, it's His Birthday!' The store, together with its parking area, covers a huge lot and driving there really is like arriving at Christmas land. Huge Santa mileposts show visitors the way and a life-size Christmas crib dominates the side of the building. But when you go inside, then the wonderland begins: acres of sparkling decorations, animated figures and Christmas cribs assault your senses. Carols and songs play and you are quite likely to be greeted by one of the Bronner family or extended family of staff in their distinctive red blazers.

There seems to be nothing which you cannot find here, whether it's books or music, ornaments or collectibles, many signed by the artists. Or you can just look at this wonderful exhibition of Christmas, including Christmas cribs from dozens of countries, all so different in style.

Outside is a full-size replica of the Silent Night Chapel in Oberndorf, Austria, where the carol 'Silent Night' is said to have originated. The Bronners have the singular honour of Oberndorf's permission to have this chapel, which has carols and services.

All over America townsfolk open their towns and doors to visitors at Christmas time, many displaying pioneer and Victorian period Christmases. The whole country becomes a huge Christmas exhibition. Christmas in America

The first American image of Santa Claus, by T. Boyd.

is like Christmas nowhere else, and the American people embrace Christmas by taking joy from simple activities and welcoming everyone in a way much of the Old World has lost and most of the New World has never achieved.

Colonial American Gingerbread

Gingerbread has been associated with Christmas all over Europe for centuries. Different groups took their recipes to America – British, Dutch, German, Polish, etc. Thus the European custom became an American one, part of the reason being that gingerbread could be kept for long periods without deteriorating. In colonial America this was very useful, when many stores were put by for a whole season.

Ingredients:
4 cups strong flour
1 cup melted butter
1 cup sugar
1 cup pure molasses
1 vanilla pod crushed and steeped overnight in
   a cup of single cream or full milk
grated rind and juice of one lemon
2 teaspoons ginger
1 teaspoon nutmeg
1 teaspoon cinnamon
1 teaspoon baking powder
1 teaspoon salt

Method:

Combine all dry ingredients except flour and mix well. Melt butter with cream, strained of its vanilla pod, and the molasses. Add the lemon. Mix. Add flour gradually, stirring all time. The dough should be stiff enough to handle without sticking to your fingers. If it does, add just a little more flour. Knead for a smooth texture. Roll out to an inch thick on a floured surface, and cut with whatever shapes you wish. Bake on a floured board at 375°F for about twelve minutes. They should spring back to the touch, but will harden as they cool.

Turrón de avellana

A SPECIALITY FROM MALLORCA

Turrón is a nutty sweet eaten in Spain, and especially associated with Christmas. It is usually made with almonds or even peanuts, but in Mallorca they have a local speciality made with roasted hazelnuts which is rich and delicious. The little shop in El Sindicato (an ancient street in Palma) where I used to buy my turrón *some thirty-five years ago had its own recipe which is reproduced here.*

Ingredients:

10 oz hazelnuts which have been roasted until the skins rub off and the nut is a pale golden colour
2 oz almonds, also roasted
3 large egg whites
6 oz set honey
6 oz fine sugar (caster sugar is best)
1 teaspoon ground cinnamon
Rice paper

Method:

First line a baking or Swiss-roll tray with enough rice paper to cover. Put all the roasted nuts into a clean teatowel and rub until the skins come off, then grind finely in a food processor or coffee grinder.

In a clean dry bowl whisk the egg whites until stiff, as for meringue. Fold into the nuts. Cover with cloth and leave in a cool place (but not a fridge) while you melt the honey and sugar together in a heavy bottomed pan. Bring to boil, but do not allow to continue boiling. Add the nut mixture and continue to cook over a low heat for about 10–12 minutes. Stir all the time so the mixture does not stick or crystallize.

Turn out on to the prepared tin, spread out neatly and cover with more rice paper, or you can use baking parchment. Leave overnight to go cold and set. Remove top paper and sprinkle with cinnamon. Cut into squares and serve with coffee as a sweetmeat after dinner.

Markets, Gingerbreads and Glass Baubles

AN ACCOUNT FROM THE NATIVITIST (1985) OF OLD CHRISTMAS IN GERMANY COMBINED WITH LOCAL STORIES

The Christmas markets throughout Europe, and particularly in Germany, are very popular events and have been so for about the past 500 years.

The most popular of all is the market in Nuremberg, which attracts thousands of visitors from all over the world – in 1988 there were over two million. Nuremberg is only a small market town, and one wonders how people moved around!

The market square is most attractive with a fountain in its centre, and flanked by the old church on one side, a superb year-round Christmas shop on another and the old walled town area on the third. The walled area has been turned into a medieval-style Christmas market, which is open all the year round too. It dates from 1559, when it was first mentioned in the Mayor's records, and was then called the Children's market.

An early nineteenth-century engraving of the children's market at Nuremberg.

It was a market based on the craftsmen's retail trade, and all the Nuremberg craftsmen displayed regularly. Many toys and gifts for children were sold at these markets, which is why they got their name, 'Kindlein' or little children's markets.

Christmas decorations as such did not appear until about 150 years ago. However, there is a story that the bakers who made the vast quantities of gingerbreads and 'Lebkuchens', which were sold at these fairs, began to use the wax from the honey used to sweeten the cakes to make angel shapes, scrolls, etc. for people to take home as a souvenir of the fair. People also bought the gilded and painted gingerbreads to hang on their Christmas trees, a custom which was popular in Germany as far back as 1600.

The market lists of 1737 show the list of craftspeople and stallholders that Christmas. There were the Alabasterers who made dolls' heads and other models; the Dollmaker who would make the famous Nuremberg 'Rauschgoldengel', which were fairy dolls dressed in pleated and gilded tinfoil; the Woodturner, who would repair a chairleg or make a wooden toy with equal skill.

The domestic craftspeople who provided services for people who used this time of year to replace their cracked plates, sharpen their knives, replace old wooden utensils were all there – the Brassbeater, the Chainsmith, the Goldsmith, the Knifesmith, the Basketworker and the Porcelain Dealer.

Also the Wax modeller, whose main trade was candles, would make wax dolls, the heads for the Tinsmith who made the 'Rauschgoldengels', and the Christmas Tree 'Fairings'. And a very important character at the Christmas Fair, the 'Lebkuchener' – the baker who made the Lebkuchen gingerbreads.

In Nuremberg, the baker's shop was established in a side road off the square as early as the mid-seventeenth century. No doubt he would bring constant supplies from his shop to the stall in the square, the warm spicy smells bringing the shoppers queuing at his booth then just as they crowd around the same shop today. The origin of the Lebkuchen recipe is said to have been in a convent in Tegernsee in Bavaria in the eleventh century.

It was to these Christmas markets, especially the one at Coburg, that the womenfolk of the Lauscha Glassblowers took the glass 'Kugeln' to be sold, in the mid-1800s, thus beginning the massive Christmas glass-ornament industry which has developed to the present time. The glassblowing industry was at that time purely domestic – beads for chandeliers, domestic vessels and so on. The story told by the old glassblowers at the factory is as follows:

Traditional Glassblowing is very thirsty work. In times past, the glass was blown over open fires lit across a yard. To get the glass to blow evenly and without bursting was very skilled work. The men would drink a lot of ale to quench their thirst, and at the end of the day, merry with ale, they would 'play' with the left-over bits of glass, blowing huge balls to see who could blow the biggest before they burst – a sort of macho competition! Later, the womenfolk would collect up the good glass spheres, and silver them with a lead compound, and take them to market to sell.

They would pack the baubles into huge wickerwork baskets, which they would carry on their backs as they walked the miles to market.

The markets exist today in most European cities. Certainly German towns large and small all have their 'Christkindmarkt', which start in early December and last right up to Christmas Eve.

The Legend of Pannetone *and the* Recipe

An Italian Christmas cake

There was once, in fifteenth-century Milan, a well-loved baker called Antonio, whose bread reached the attentions of a nobleman. Toni delivered his bread daily to the nobleman's house and fell in love with the daughter of this great man. But he could not approach her because he was too poor.

There was a very special bread, expensive and only made for great feast days. This bread was a sweet yeast cake called Cherubini. *Toni developed a variation of this bread using the very new sweetmeats, candied peels and sultanas. It was an instant hit and soon Toni became famous for his bread, which became known as Toni's bread, or in Italian* Pannetoni. *He became rich and won his noble lady. Today Pannetone is associated with all the major feasts, but especially Christmas.*

Ingredients:

2 oz caster sugar

1 oz fresh yeast or 3 teaspoons dried

1 pt lukewarm water

3 egg yolks

1 teaspoon vanilla essence

1 teaspoon grated lemon rind

1 teaspoon salt

14 oz plain white flour

4 oz of butter (works well with low-fat spreads too)

2 oz sultanas

2 oz chopped peel

1 oz melted butter

Method:

Make up the yeast according to the instructions. Beat egg yolks in bowl, add frothy yeast mixture, vanilla, rind, salt and sugar. Beat in half of flour, then gradually the melted butter and finally the rest of the flour. If you use a mixer, have it on slow. You should now have a very elastic dough. Turn on to a floured board and knead for 10 minutes until firm and still elastic. Set in a warm place for about 1 hour to rise to twice its size.

Preheat your oven 200°C/400°F/Gas 6. Knead risen dough again, this time kneading in the sultanas and candied peel. Place in a deep cake tin lined with non-stick baking parchment. Leave again to rise to the top of the tin. Brush top with melted butter. Bake for 20 minutes. Reduce oven to 180°C/350°F/Gas 5, brush cake again with butter, continue cooking for 45 minutes more. Brush a third time with the melted butter and continue the cooking for another 30 minutes.

Remove on to rack to cool, brush on any remaining butter. Serve when cold, slice thinly and serve with coffee.

Kuskus – an Israeli Ancestor of Plum Pudding?

Long ago Hebrew schoolboys were served with a delicious concoction called kuskus, *which is related to* kutia *in Poland,* muga *in the Viking North and 'moggy' in Northern England. Not to be confused with* couscous *as served elsewhere in the Mediterranean world,* kuskus *is an early form of the plum porridge served in old England, and the forerunner of Christmas pudding. Kuskus was a special treat at Hanukka and the idea may have been brought to England by the*

Crusaders. The ingredients sound a little unusual to Western ears, but with fruits, meat and grains being commonly eaten now in curries it is worth including here – and absolutely delicious.

Ingredients:

1 cup coarsely milled whole-wheat (you can use a coffee grinder or processor)

2 cups boiling water

1 teaspoon salt

2 tablespoons oil or chicken fat

1 diced onion

1 lb ground lean lamb

4 oz chopped celery

1 cup raisins

1 cup sweet wine

2 tablespoons honey

Method:

Toast wheat lightly in non-stick frying pan, stirring until dry and lightly browned. Pour in salted water, cover and simmer on a low heat for half an hour. Put into a large 6 pt dish. Heat oil or fat in frypan, add onion and meat and brown; add all remaining ingredients, cook them lightly, put into the dish with the toasted grain, mixing well. Cover dish and bake in moderate oven about 350°F for about 45 minutes, adding liquid or chicken or vegetable stock to keep moist if it starts to dry out. Serves 4–6.

GIFT-GIVING AND RECEIVING

Santa Claus Came from Turkey

AND THE GOLDEN FOAL – ANCIENT TRANSYLVANIAN GIFTBRINGER

Gülsen Kahraman

Turkey, even to the Turks, is not the first place to spring to mind in association with not only Christmas but also the most popular Christmas figure. But Demre in Turkey was the place where St Nicholas, Bishop of Myra, came from. Most of Turkey follows the religion of Islam and only in a small area are there Christians, who tend to be Orthodox. Their customs are similar to those of Greece. But, from Turkey comes the story of St Nicholas.

This is a true story about Santa Claus. Santa Claus is, of course, a short way of saying St Nicholas; and St Nicholas was not born, as you may think, in a land of snow and igloos. The real St Nicholas was born long ago in a land of green hills, warm sun and soft sea breezes. He was born in the ancient village of Patara on the southern shore of Turkey.

When Nicholas grew to be a young man his parents died and left him a great deal of money. Instead of spending the money on himself, Nicholas gave his money away whenever he saw somebody who was poor and in need of help. Young Nicholas would also be very careful that he helped people in secret. That was the right way to do a good deed, he felt, in secret without expecting credit or thanks.

There is one special story which has been told for years which best shows Nicholas' special love for young people and his fondness for giving gifts in secret. It is because of this story that many years later presents are still being given to children as a surprise and a secret at Christmas. Here is the story:

Near Nicholas' home in the town of Patara lived a poor nobleman who had three beautiful daughters. The family lived in a very shabby palace and had hardly enough to eat. Even worse, the three daughters wanted to get married but there was no money with which to give them a wedding. And in those days it was quite impossible to marry off a daughter unless there was enough money to give her a wedding. Things were going from bad to worse for the three daughters and their father. When things were just about as bad as they could be, young Nicholas heard about the family and decided to help them.

One night when it was dark, Nicholas went to the shabby palace of this poor nobleman, and threw a bag of gold through the window and ran away before he could be seen. The nobleman and his daughters were very surprised and happy. But the next morning Nicholas was not happy because he thought he had been stingy with his gift. The poor nobleman had three daughters ready to be married, but he, Nicholas, had only given them enough money to pay for the wedding of one of them. Sure enough, on another dark night soon after, Nicholas threw another bag of gold into the nobleman's room and again ran away without being seen. But he still had not given enough gold.

He went back on a third dark night, but he could not throw the gold through the palace window this time because all the windows were now repaired. Then Nicholas had the idea of climbing up on the palace roof and throwing the bag of gold down the chimney. Earlier that night, the three daughters had washed their stockings and hung them up to dry near the chimney and when Nicholas tossed the bag down the chimney the gold fell into their stockings. With all the gold the three daughters were happily married and lived a very good life. And when years later Nicholas became a very holy and famous man, people remembered this story and put their empty stockings out at night and surprisingly found them filled the next morning.

Nicholas, of course, did not know that he had begun a custom that would last perhaps forever. He did not even think about his good deed, but just went about his business living his life as best he could.

An artist's representation of the young St Nicholas.

Nicholas, as was the habit among religious Christians of his day, went on a visit to the Holy Land. After his stay in Jerusalem he decided not to return to his home but went to live in the town of Myra (which today is called Demre) because it was an important centre of Christian faith.

Early one morning he went into church as he did every day and was surprised to see all the churchmen gathered ahead of him. They ran up to him shouting, 'Hail to our new Bishop'; Nicholas could hardly believe his ears. The churchmen explained, 'Our old Bishop died a few days ago. We have been arguing ever since about who should be chosen to take his place but we could not agree. Last night as we prayed we heard a voice which said, "Choose as your Bishop the first man who shall enter the church in the morning." We have spent all night here and now our prayers have been answered. You were the first to enter the church. Hail to Nicholas, Bishop of Myra!'

And so it was done. Nicholas became Bishop of Myra and he remained the amazing man he had always been. He performed many miracles in his lifetime; and he was well loved and respected by the people who knew him and the people who only heard stories of his goodness. Nicholas was so well loved that the citizens built a church in his honour. The Church of St Nicholas is still there, but because the church was very near the river, years of floods left layers of sand all round the church. The people of Demre have always kept the doorway to the church cleared, but you must climb down a flight of stairs to reach it.

It was many years later, when another church was built in Italy in honour of St Nicholas, that stories of his life were told to European children. On the eve of St Nicholas' Day, children would leave their shoes and stockings out and because St Nicholas loved children, there would always be presents left in secret for the children in his honour. Although St Nicholas' Day is 6 December, the parties and presents of that day lasted until Christmas and soon became part of the Christmas spirit.

It is hard for us today to find Santa Claus in any one place because there are children everywhere and everywhere the spirit of Santa Claus must be to surprise them with secret gifts. But if you ever visit the village of Demre, you will know you are visiting the place where St Nicholas lived. And if you visit this village in Turkey at Christmas time you will hear the people say, '*Qok mutlu b ir Noel gec irmen iz i d idler im*' – which is the Turkish way of saying, 'Have a very merry Christmas'.

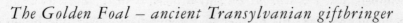
A Matter of Presents

An extract from Little Women by Louisa May Alcott

Louisa May Alcott was born in Pennsylvania, America in 1932. She wrote her popular novel Little Women *in 1868. In this short extract from one of America's most famous stories, we join the 'Little Women' making their plans for Christmas despite the financial problems they are encountering while their father is away in the army. The four girls have been discussing what they would like for Christmas and what they should give, with their limited budgets. Their mother has just suggested that no presents be expected due to their difficulties. The conversation begins with Jo grumbling that 'Christmas won't be Christmas without any presents'. Meg suggests that if they all make little sacrifices, they could manage something. But Jo wants to buy herself a longed-for book with her dollar, while Beth wants to buy music and Amy the artist says she will buy drawing pencils. But later, while putting their Mamma's slippers to warm by the fire, they notice how worn out they are. So plans are made for a shopping trip, and some parlour theatricals.*

The clock struck six; and, having swept up the hearth, Beth put a pair of slippers down to warm. Somehow the sight of the old shoes had a good effect upon the girls; for mother was coming, and everyone brightened to welcome her. Meg stopped lecturing, and lighted the lamp. Amy got out of the easy chair without being asked, and Jo forgot how tired she was as she sat up to hold the slippers nearer to the blaze.

'They are quite worn out; Marmee must have a new pair.'

'I thought I'd get her some with my dollar,' said Beth.

'No, I shall!' cried Amy.

'I'm the oldest,' began Meg, but Jo cut in with a decided – 'I'm the man of the family now papa is away, and *I* shall provide the slippers, for he told me to take special care of mother while he was gone.'

'I'll tell you what we'll do,' said Beth; 'let's each get her something for Christmas, and not get anything for ourselves.'

'That's like you, dear! What will we get?' exclaimed Jo.

Everyone thought soberly for a minute; then Meg announced, as if the idea was suggested by the sight of her own pretty hands, 'I shall give her a nice pair of gloves.'

'Army shoes, best to be had,' cried Jo.

'Some handkerchiefs, all hemmed,' said Beth.

'I'll get a little bottle of cologne; she likes it, and it won't cost much, so I'll have some left to buy my pencils,' added Amy.

'How will we give the things?' asked Meg.

'Put them on the table, and bring her in and see her open the bundles. Don't you remember how we used to do on our birthdays?' answered Jo.

'I used to be *so* frightened when it was my turn to sit in the big chair with the crown on, and see you all coming marching round to give the presents, with a kiss. I liked the things and the kisses, but it was dreadful to have you sit looking at me while I opened the bundles,' said Beth, who was toasting her face and the bread for tea, at the same time.

'Let Marmee think we are getting things for ourselves, and then surprise her. We must go shopping tomorrow afternoon. Meg; there is so much to do about the play for Christmas night,' said Jo, marching up and down, with her hands behind her back and her nose in the air.

'I don't mean to act any more after this; I'm getting too old for such things,' observed Meg, who was as much a child as ever about 'dressing-up' frolics.

'You won't stop, I know, as long as you can trail round in a white gown with your hair down, and wear gold-paper jewelry. You are the best actress we've got, and there'll be an end of everything if you quit the boards,' said Jo. 'We ought to rehearse tonight. Come here, Amy, and do the fainting scene, for you are as stiff as a poker in that.'

'I can't help it; I never saw anyone faint, and I don't choose to make myself all black and blue, tumbling flat as you do. If I can go down easily, I'll drop; if I can't, I shall fall into a chair and be graceful; I don't care if Hugo does come at me with a pistol,' returned Amy, who was not gifted with dramatic power, but was chosen because she was small enough to be borne out shrieking by the villain of the piece.

'Do it this way; clasp your hands so, and stagger across the room, crying frantically, "Roderigo! save me! save me!"' and away went Jo, with a melodramatic scream which was truly thrilling.

Amy followed, but she poked her hands out stiffly before her, and jerked herself along as if she went by machinery; and her 'Ow!' was more suggestive of pins being run into her than of fear and anguish. Jo gave a despairing groan, and Meg laughed outright, while Beth let her bread burn as she watched the fun, with interest.

'It's no use! Do the best you can when the time comes, and if the audience laughs, don't blame me. Come on, Meg.'

Then things went smoothly, for Don Pedro defied the world in a speech of two pages wihout a single break; Hagar, the witch, chanted an awful incantation over her kettleful of simmering toads, with weird effect; Roderigo rent his chains asunder manfully, and Hugo died in agonies of remorse and arsenic, with a wild 'Ha! ha!'

'It's the best we've had yet,' said Meg, as the dead villain sat up and rubbed his elbows.

'I don't see how you can write and act such splendid things, Jo. You're a regular Shakespeare!' exclaimed Beth, who firmly believed that her sisters were gifted with wonderful genius in all things.

'Not quite,' replied Jo modestly. 'I do think "The Witch's Curse, an Operatic Tragedy" is rather a nice thing; but I'd like to try "Macbeth," if we only had a trap door for Banquo. I always wanted to do the killing part. "Is that a dagger that I see before me?"' muttered Jo, rolling her eyes and clutching at the air, as she had seen a famous tragedian do.

'No, it's the toasting fork, with mother's shoe on it instead of the bread. Beth's stage-struck!' cried Meg, and the rehearsal ended in a general burst of laughter.

A Drum for Christmas in Guyana

N o r m a n   B e a t o n

The late and sadly missed Norman Beaton was a pioneer in black comedy as the sharp-tongued hero of the comedy series Desmond. *I had the privilege of meeting him during the filming of a* Kilroy *Christmas special programme which investigated (appropriately enough) the worldwide adaptations of Christmas. After the programme we talked extensively about his early memories. Reproduced below is his funny account of a childhood Christmas in Guyana.*

Christmas for me as a child in Guyana was a time of scents. Ginger and other spices would have been drying outside for some time. The quality of light changed, and we could sense a thrill in the air. All the mothers would prepare many different kinds of food depending on how much money they had. Poultry that had been scratching around outside would disappear only to be reborn on the table. I seem to remember that Guinea fowl were popular.

It really was a festival of food. We did not have the shopping opportunities that are a feature of the English Christmas. Everybody would be cooking both sweet and savoury dishes with a variety of spices and the smell was everywhere. We all used to get very excited.

We were in no sense rich, but we didn't know any different. There was always plenty of food and it was much appreciated. My mother would spend almost the whole Christmas time cooking, while my father having no work to do would sit out Christmas Day in the company of a bottle of rum. (Most men were banished from the house by their wives when there was a great deal of cooking to do.) The men usually made their own entertainment at Christmas time and for entertainment read drinking, and for drinking read rum.

On this particular Christmas, my father had been out for most of Christmas Eve drinking with his friends. The effects of this were increased by a few drinks after the Christmas lunch, and he had gone to ground in the bedroom like a bear sleeping off toothache.

I had been very lucky. I had found in my stocking a shiny tin drum. As this was my best present (it was my only present!) I was determined to make full use of it. I went round the house banging it until my mother told me to go outside. So I went out banging it along the road, back in the garden, under the bedroom window when . . . some kind of mad bear-like animal whirlwind exploded, it hurtled out of the house making some kind of roar and grabbed my drum. I was there with my drumstick poised ready to hit and it was gone . . . With so much rum inside him, my father was not a music lover!

St Nicholas Rides a White Horse

Today St Nicholas comes to the shores of Amsterdam by boat, legend has it, from Spain, where he rescued the little Moorish slave boy, Peter. He comes on 6 December and brings all manner of good things for the children.

However, a good few years ago, I picked up a dog-eared old book at the famous flea market in Amsterdam. Minus cover, minus title page, but with lovely pictures, it tells the story of a naughty little girl, Kersti, living in Zeeland, who is always getting up to mischief. Now in Holland, the naughty children get birch twigs left in their shoes as a warning to be good from the sack carried by Black Peter, so when Kersti steals all the Christmas sweets and is sent to bed without supper and without seeing the good Bishop, her sisters fear the worst for her.

This story illustrates the traditions of St Nicholas in Holland at the beginning of the twentieth century.

Kersti had cried herself to sleep, but all the sweets she had eaten made her restless and she woke up in the middle of the night. She remembered that something terrible had happened. Oh, yes, she had not been allowed to put out her clog. 'Now St Nicholas will think I am dead and he won't leave me anything,' she muttered, a tear falling on her blanket. 'I know what I'll do, I'll go out and find him and tell him I'm not dead.'

She dressed herself and tiptoed past her peacefully breathing sisters. By the door she slipped on her clogs and her shawl and stepped out into the dark snowy world. It was cold and the moon in the sky looked like a snowball that had been thrown up and would not come down. Never before had Kersti been out alone

In Holland the giftbringer appears in his traditional garb as a bishop. Courtesy of the Nederlands Tourist Board.

like this in the middle of the night when shadows were long and dark. But she wanted to find St Nicholas, so she pulled her shawl closer and went on bravely.

She stepped on the frozen canal and almost fell, it was so slippy. A wind blew on her back, and spreading her skirts like sails, she sailed along, faster and faster. She slid under arched bridges, glided past windmills and houses until she arrived in town.

'Where is St Nicholas now?' she thought. 'If he does not hurry up the night will be gone.' She peeped down a street where the houses leaned over, the roofs almost meeting. . . . Just as she turned a corner she saw St Nicholas and stood still, too much in awe to speak.

There he was on a white horse, tall and splendid in the moonlight, a mitre on his head and a staff of gold over his shoulder. After him toiled Pieterbaas,

carrying a heavy bag. Kersti remembered all the bad things she shouldn't have done, and all the good things she might have done. She looked at St Nicholas' eyes, and took courage. They were kind eyes. But when St Nicholas spoke, his voice was gruff.

'Who is that little girl and why is she not in bed?' he asked.

'Don't you know me?' asked Kersti in surprise. 'I'm Kersti . . . and I want a cookstove, with a real fire in it and a house made of sweets like Hansel and Gretel found, and a dress of gold.'

'Are you taking this down?' St Nicholas motioned to Pieterbaas . . .

'. . . and Bettkee wants a new necklace of red beads because hers broke,' Kersti continued, 'and Mintje would like a sewing basket and Gerda and Truda want a book – and I want that too – with coloured pictures please . . .'

'And what about your mother and father?'

'They've got me!' she said simply.

'Write it down, write it down, Pieterbaas. Don't forget anything.'

'It's all right by me suh,' he grumbled, thumbing through his notebook, 'But I got down here that this Kersti is a bad child and should have the birch rod.'

'Let me see,' said St Nicholas '. . . ah, here we are . . . oh dear, oh dear, what a list of wickedness. And she stole! She stole sweets from her mother. No, I'm afraid you will have to scratch out those wishes of hers, Pieterbaas'.

Naughty Kersti stamped her foot. 'If you do that, I'll tell everyone you are not a saint, that you are just an ordinary man without any hair . . . and with crooked legs!'

Here the story has some pages torn and missing, but the storyline follows that the good saint is very distressed with naughty Kersti and even more so when Pieterbaas says that she does not say her prayers! Pieterbaas recommends the birch twigs be left in her clog as a reminder to be better next year. But the goodly saint decides that here is a child who is the youngest unwanted girl of a large group of daughters so he decides to give her a treat to encourage her to be better. He takes her around all the chimneys, and gives in to her pleading that the naughty children should have a present to make them better!

The next morning she awakens in her bed to find that St Nicholas has left all the presents she asked for for her sisters and did not forget to leave the 'real cooking stove' for Kersti herself.

Gaghant Bata – the Armenian Giftbringer

On New Year's Day, this Santa Claus-like character came to give gifts to old and young alike. Armenian housewives prepared for his coming by baking huge trays of treats made from recipes which have been handed down from times forgotten, treats which have been traditional to Gaghant for centuries. There is a cake with a cross or a bird on it, and a sweetmeat consisting of nuts and syrup made from grapes. After the Gaghant welcoming meal, there is singing and dancing in the streets and the children go singing around the houses where they are rewarded with fruits, nuts and other sweetmeats.

Carol singing at the neighbours' houses.

Icelandic Lads

All the Scandinavian countries have small gnome-like creatures, house spirits, for which they observe a certain respect. A saucer of milk or a bowl of porridge is said to keep them happy and mischief-free.

The Icelandic Lads are also known as the Yule Host, and come from a belief that the spirits of the unbaptised dead roam the skies at Christmas time. The book, *Giftbringers of the World*, describes them as 'A motley

The Icelandic Lads, from The Giftbringers, *1985.*

crew of spirits . . . with such names as "Skirt Blower"; "Latch Rattler"; and "Door Sniffer". Their names describing their chief activities throughout the year. Thus the actions of the wind will be put down to "skirt blower" or "latch rattler" for instance.

However, on Christmas Eve they put aside their pranks and take on the role of Giftbringers to Icelandic children who are admonished to be good in case "Window Peeker" is watching, and they change their giftbringing into mischiefmaking!'

Acknowledgements

I would like to thank the following people and organizations for their help in researching this book:

Barbara Koscielny, the Polish Cultural Attaché; Marian Dabrosky, Polish advisor of culture and science; Austrian Tourist Board; Mr Eli Rosen, former attaché to the Israeli Cultural Ministry; Wallace Bronner of Bronner's Christmas Wonderland; ENIT, the Italian Information Centre; Ministry of Foreign Affairs, Helsinki, Finland; Finnish Tourist Board, Rovaneimi; Press and Cultural Relations Department of the Ministry of Foreign Affairs of Denmark; the Mexican Embassy, London; the Austrian Institute, London; the Swiss Embassy, London; the Embassy of Brazil; the Belgian Embassy, London; Archbishop Gregorius of the Coptic Church, Egypt; the Philippine Embassy; Bryan Foster of Sweden; Klara Johnson of Minnesota; Mrs Eirwen Jones of Pontadawe; Dr Nina Gockerell of the Bavarian National Museum, Munich; the James Cook Museum; Diana Jarvis Reeves of the Canadian High Commission; Dr Attila Selmeczi Kovca, Ethnographic Museum, Budapest; Pablo Casals; José Meneze; Helena de Pettes; Ministry of Education and Culture, Commonwealth of Bahamas; Mrs Mary Turner, Leeds; Norman Beaton; Lee Butterfield of the Putz Committee, First Moravian Church of Bethlehem, Pennsylvania; Mariko Okawa, Cultural Officer of the Felissimo Christmas Museum, Hakodate Japan; Akio Onishi; Emelia von Staufer; Mr Hirokatsu Onishi of Gifu Prefecture; Mrs Masako Onishi, Gifu Kindergarten; the Japanese Information Centre, London; Margaret Ferguson, Scotland; Mrs Margaret Tait of Lerwick, Shetland; Mrs Marie Kathleen Lenihan; Staff and workers at the Lauscha Glass Museum and Factory, Thuringia; The *Shetland Times* and Mr Jim Nicholson, editor of *Shetland Life* for permission to reproduce '*Dir nae Christmas noo*' and the 'Shetland Calendar' from the December 1981 issue; the White House Help Desk; the Internet – the First Lady's Home Page; the Internet – the Polish Polar Station, Antarctica; the Internet – Central Valley Christian School, USA.

I have used the following books and newspapers in my research:

A Wayfarer in Poland, Monica Gardner, 1917; The Augsburg Christmas Annual; *Poland Today*, Ministry Foreign Affairs, Warsaw; *Christmas Time in Many a Clime*,

CMS, 1905; *The Journal of the Society of Nativitists*, vols 3, 4 and 10; *The Journal of the Society of Nativitists*, Midsummer, 1990; Christmas, 1989; 'The Nativitist', Midsummer 1988 for my translation of 'Carol of the Birds', 1988; *Routledge's Annual*, 1885; *Giftbringers of the World*, European Folk Study Centre 1985; *Christmas in Many Lands*, Okeden & Welsh, 1888; *Illustrated Melbourne Post*, 22 December 1864; *A Canadian Christmas Carol*, the Huronia Historic Development Council, 1967; Lydia Goshgarih of the Hamilton and District Multicultural Centre; *Christmas Lasts Forever*, Hannen Foss, 1945; *A Versailles Christmastide*, Mary Stuart Boyd, pub. Chatto & Windus, 1901; *Legenda Sancti Francisci*; Thomas de Celano, 1229–57; *Domitor*, Tekla, Budapest, 1972; The Catholic *Universe* newspaper; *Christmas with the Washingtons*, Olive Bailey, Dietz, 1948; *New York Times*, 1910–81; *The White House at Christmastime*; *Christian Advocate*, 17 December 1931; And many other American publications and newspapers which have been used for research.

I am grateful to the following people for their assistance in translating material:

Emelia von Staufer (Japanese); Akio Onishi (Japanese); Andrew Hubert von Staufer (German, French, Dutch, Swedish); Kazimir Hubert (Russian, Hungarian and Czech). Latin, Provençal, Spanish and Catalan translations are by myself.

I thank the following people and organizations for providing illustrations and for permission to reproduce them in this book:

The Polish Cultural Attaché; Bronner's Christmas Wonderland; Christmas Archives Picture Library; the Salzburger Museum, Salzburg, Austria; the Finnish Tourist Board; the Spanish Tourist Board; the Netherlands Tourist Board; the Danish Ministry of Foreign Affairs; Bayerische Nationalmuseum, Munich; ENIT; the Cultural Attaché for Ontario, the Canadian High Commission; the Lauscha Glass Museum; the Huron Historical Development Council; the Society of Nativitists; Helena de Pettes; Mrs Onishi.

Many of the first-hand accounts and some of the illustrations reproduced in this book were collected up to twenty years ago, and consequently it has not been possible to make contact with all the contributors. As most were given freely with the hope of future publication, I hope that my kind contributors will take this as a promise honoured. Should any wish to get in touch, please write care of the publisher. All unacknowledged pieces are by myself.